A HANDBOOK OF Spoken Grammar

STRATEGIES FOR SPEAKING NATURAL ENGLISH

School of
English Studies
Folkestone

26 Grimston Gardens, Folkestone
Kent CT20 2PX, England
Tel: 01303 850007 Fax: 01303 256544
Email: info@ses-folkestone.co.uk
Internet: www.ses-folkestone.co.uk

Ken Paterson
Caroline Caygill and
Rebecca Sewell

DELTA PUBLISHING

DELTA Publishing
Quince Cottage
Hoe Lane
Peaslake
Surrey GU5 9SW
England
www.deltapublishing.co.uk

Text © Ken Paterson, Caroline Caygill and Rebecca Sewell
Design and layout © Delta Publishing 2011

The right of Ken Paterson, Caroline Caygill and Rebecca Sewell to be identified as authors of this work has been asserted by them in accordance with the Copyright, Designs and Patents Act, 1988.

All rights reserved. No reproduction, copy or transmission of this publication may be made without written permission from the publishers or in accordance with the provisions of the Copyright, Designs and Patents Act 1988, or under the terms of any licence permitting copying issued by the Copyright Licensing Agency, 90 Tottenham Court Road, London W1P 9HE.

First published 2011
Edited by Tanya Whatling
Designed by DJHunterDesign
Cartoons by Adam Larkum/illustrationweb

Cover design by DJHunterDesign
Audio production by Ian Harker

Printed in Malta by Melita Press

Acknowledgments
The authors would like to thank Nick Boisseau at DELTA for helping to transform an enthusiasm into a book, and Tanya Whatling, our editor, for her care and her incisive comments. We would also like to acknowledge a debt to the Longman Grammar of Spoken and Written English by Biber, Johansson, Leech, Conrad and Finegan (Longman 1999) and to Ronald Carter and Michael McCarthy for all their work on spoken grammar, but specifically for the Cambridge Grammar of English (CUP 2006).

ISBN 978-1-905085-54-5

CONTENTS

		Page
	Map of the book	4
	Introduction	6

Unit

1	Short questions for everyday conversations	8
2	Common structures with *know* and *think*	12
3	Modify meaning with *actually, really, of course*, etc.	16
4	Improve your naming skills	20
5	Send signals with *I mean, you see, you know*, etc.	24
6	Use *so* and *do* to make effective responses	28
7	Sound more polite	32
8	Be vague with *thing/thingy, and things (like that)*, etc.	36
9	Be vague with *sort of, kind of, a couple of*, etc.	40
10	Say less	44
11	Exaggerate!	48
12	How to use *oh, ah, wow, ouch*, etc.	52
13	Make statements work as questions	56
14	Report speech in a more immediate way	60
15	Use *had better*, *have got to* and *be supposed to* correctly	64
16	Make short responses to agree or show interest	68
17	Add verb, adverb and adjective pairs	72
18	Follow your partner	76
19	Put important things at the front	80
20	Put important things at the end	84
	Key	88

MAP OF THE BOOK

UNIT 1 — Short questions for everyday conversations

Quite often we only use the endings of questions, or we use very short questions with *about* or with prepositions.

- A: *More tea?*
- B: Yes, please. Half a cup is fine, though.
- A: I've been looking for a new job.
- B: Oh. *Any luck?*

UNIT 2 — Common structures with *know* and *think*

Some short structures or patterns of words are used again and again in spoken English as a 'springboard' for sentences.

- A: *I don't know what* to do today.
- B: Why don't we have a game of tennis?
- A: Who paid for the hotel?
- B: I'm not sure. *I think it was* Jaci.

UNIT 3 — Modify meaning with *actually, really, of course*, etc.

In conversation we often do more than simply express a basic meaning. Sometimes, for example, we also show our 'attitude' to what we're saying.

- A: Are you *actually* going out in that rain?
- B: *Of course.* I've got to get to work, haven't I?
- A: I shouldn't have criticised you like that in front of everyone. I'm sorry.
- B: It's alright, *really*. I don't mind. I'd rather people said what they thought.

UNIT 4 — Improve your naming skills

There are three main ways of addressing people: by first name; by title (e.g. *Mr Smith*); and by general words such as *guys*.

- A: Where are we eating, *guys*?
- B: I'm not sure, *Mike*. They say the Italian place is good.
- A: Shall we meet at the cinema, *Jay*?
- B: Alright, *Meg*. Is that okay with you, *Pete*?

UNIT 5 — Send signals with *I mean, you see, you know*, etc.

Sometimes, in conversation, we use a word or short phrase to 'signal' the type of thing we're about to say or we've just said.

- A: …and then in the afternoon, we're going to climb all three mountains.
- B: *Right*. That sounds like fun.
- A: But I thought you liked really spicy food.
- B: *Well*, I don't. I've told you before.

UNIT 6 — Use *so* and *do* to make effective responses

So and *do* have many uses in English. They both play an important part, for example, in the business of 'connecting' bits of conversation together.

- A: Olivia and Jack are getting married.
- B: *So* I heard. It's great news.
- A: Have you e-mailed your boss?
- B: Yes, I *have done*, but she hasn't replied.

UNIT 7 — Sound more polite

Being polite means making your language less direct (often through past tenses) – and knowing how to respond to what other people say.

- A: *Excuse me*, I think you've dropped your gloves!
- B: *Oh dear!* I'm always doing that. *Thanks very much.*
- A: *You're welcome.* Would you like a hand with your bags?
- B: Yes, *please. I'm afraid* they're quite heavy. Do you live round here?

UNIT 8 — Be vague with *thing/thingy*, and *things (like that)*, etc.

Spoken language is often vague. We don't always have time to be precise – and being vague can be a more relaxed way of speaking to people.

- A: Look. I've got this *thing* on my leg.
- B: You poor *thing*, Sam. Does it hurt?
- A: What do you do in the evenings?
- B: Play music, watch TV *and things like that*.

UNIT 9 — Be vague with *sort of, kind of, a couple of*, etc.

As mentioned in Unit 8, spoken language is often vague. In this unit, we look at some more vague language.

- A: What happened to you yesterday?
- B: I was feeling *kind of* ill, so I went home.
- A: Are you looking forward to the weekend?
- B: *Sort of*. I've got quite a lot of work to do, but I should get a break on Sunday.

UNIT 10 — Say less

Ellipsis means leaving out (not saying) words when your meaning is clear without them. It is a natural part of conversation, not only because it saves time, but also because it 'links' what we say to what our partner has said.

- A: Are you feeling okay?
- B: Got a headache again, I'm afraid.
- A: Where are you?
- B: On the train.

UNIT 11 — Exaggerate

Exaggerated language (sometimes called *hyperbole*) is very common in informal conversation, particularly amongst teenagers, and when we're gossiping or telling stories.

A: How's it been?
B: Really busy! *Hundreds of people rang* while you were out.
A: *These shoes are killing me!*
B: Don't worry. We'll be home soon.

UNIT 12 — How to use *oh, ah, wow, ouch*, etc.

There are a number of words – sometimes called *interjections* – that we use regularly in conversation, but hardly ever write down.

A: The problem is that my flat's too small.
B: *Oh*, I see. Well, Sue can stay with me, if you like.
A: Anyway, I decided to treat myself to a new dress. What do you think?
B: *Wow!* It's gorgeous.

UNIT 13 — Make statements work as questions

To make a statement into a question, we normally change the word order, or use *do/does/did* or a question tag. But it isn't always necessary.

A: Scott's booked a table for 6p.m.
B: We're eating before the play?
A: We'll pick Mike up on the way.
B: Mike's coming, too?

UNIT 14 — Report speech in a more immediate way

Reporting speech normally involves a process of changing tenses, pronouns and time and place words. In this unit, we focus instead on a simpler way – and a special use of the past continuous.

A: How did it go?
B: Not very well. I started by saying to him, '*Look*, if we don't find a way of working together, we'll never get the product launch ready in time.' And he said, '*Oh*, I didn't know we had a problem.' So I said, '*Well*, you haven't replied to any of my last three e-mails.'

UNIT 15 — Use *had better*, *have got to* and *be supposed to* correctly

Three modal verb phrases, which you will have seen before, are much more common in conversation than in written English: *had better*, *have got to* and *be supposed to*.

A: *Aren't you supposed to* be at work?
B: It's okay. My boss gave me the afternoon off. I've *got to* do a presentation tomorrow for some clients. The phone was ringing all the time, so she said I'*d better* go home and finish it off there.

UNIT 16 — Make short responses to agree or show interest

The way in which we respond to what people say is one of the most important parts of conversational English. In this unit, we look at using adjectives, adverbs and very short questions.

A: We can have a pizza before the film.
B: *Great*.
A: Tim's coming to the match.
B: *Excellent*. I haven't seen him for ages.

UNIT 17 — Add verb, adverb and adjective pairs

In conversation we sometimes like to use verbs, adverbs and adjectives in pairs, linked by *and*. With verbs and adverbs, it adds a sense of action and movement; with adjectives, it adds emphasis to a description.

Are you going to *come and get* this food while it's hot?
Try and do some tidying while we're out. It's your turn.
It's great here! All the shops are *nice and close*.
There are a few mistakes *here and there*, but it's a good essay in general.

UNIT 18 — Follow your partner

Conversation, unlike writing, is interactive. In this unit, we'll look at ways in which people link what they say directly to the sentence they've just heard in a conversation.

A: They shouldn't keep people waiting like this. It's terrible.
B: *You're right*. It's awful.
A: I'm full. That was a beautiful meal.
B: *Gorgeous*, wasn't it? Do you want some coffee?

UNIT 19 — Put important things at the front

In conversation, we can sometimes change the regular order of words to put emphasis on particular parts of the sentence. Here we look at 'heads': things we take from their normal place and put at the front of sentences.

A: *My new trainers*, I can't find them anywhere.
B: Have you looked under the sofa?
A: *This DVD player*, is it the cheapest one you've got?
B: No, madam. But it's one of the most popular.

UNIT 20 — Put important things at the end

In this unit, we look at 'tails': things we take from their normal place and put at the end of sentences.

A: They're rather good, *these sardines*. How's your curry?
B: Actually, I'm not very hungry. I'm feeling a bit tense.
A: Well, this is your chance to relax, *this meal with me*. I know you're worrying about your sister again. But try to be positive. She'll be okay, *Sophie will*.

INTRODUCTION

A Handbook of Spoken Grammar is a study book for intermediate to upper-intermediate students. Each unit presents one feature of spoken grammar, explains how it works and then practises it in a variety of natural conversational settings.

Spoken grammar can perhaps be defined as 'elements of natural conversation that have always existed, but have often been excluded from the traditional grammar syllabus.' Recent research has begun to identify and describe this language. The authors of this book have selected the features that they believe will be most useful to learners of English.

Spoken grammar is not the same as 'slang'. Most of the language in this book can be used in everyday conversations with all types of people – but when a certain item is particularly informal, we say so. Short recorded dialogues throughout the book help in the matter of stress and intonation.

Why learn spoken grammar?

- The features of spoken grammar help to create an easy-going, natural kind of English that is used at college and work these days, as well as with family and friends.
- Spoken grammar is often an economical grammar. For example, it's quicker to say, *Any messages?* or *Any luck?* than, *Are there any messages?* or *Did you have any luck?*
- Spoken grammar is sometimes an easy grammar. It's simpler to say to a friend, for example, *I said to Anne, 'look are you sure?'* than, *I asked Anne if she was really sure.*
- It is often a polite grammar because it gives you opportunities to be less direct. You might say to someone *What **sort of** job do you do, **then**?* rather than *What job do you do?*
- In the interplay of conversation, it gives you more choices, such as when to reveal the subject of your sentence: *It's such a wonderful place to spend a few days in, New York.*

The structure of the book

The book is made up of twenty units, each consisting of two double-page sections. The book has been arranged so that, generally speaking, the units at the beginning are easier, but otherwise it is not necessary to work through the units in any particular sequence.

After the one-page Contents list, there is a Map of the Book giving brief explanations and examples of the language so that students and teachers can find exactly what they want quickly and easily.

How the units work

The focus throughout each unit is on providing students with natural language and building their confidence in using it.

Individual units are divided into two sections. In the first, the new language is introduced in a simple way to ensure that meaning and use are clear. There are plenty of examples, including short dialogues, and practice questions (with answers) to check understanding of the main concepts. Some examples are recorded to highlight pronunciation.

In the second section, there are many different types of exercise, ensuring there is an opportunity for thorough and varied practice. These might involve filling in gaps; matching sentence beginnings and endings; putting dialogues in the right order; or rewriting phrases or sentences, using the new language. Some of the exercises are recorded, and designed to check stress and intonation. Answers to all the exercises are given in the key at the back of the book.

At the end of the second section there are short extension activities to give students extra practice in a 'freer' style.

Audio CD

The CD contains recordings of some of the key examples and dialogues. These are indicated with the ( ) symbol. Listening to the recordings helps students better understand how tone, mood and speaker intentions are expressed.

To the student

As you use this book, you will probably become more aware of spoken grammar. Once you start noticing it, you will find that is everywhere, in all kinds of contexts: on TV, in the news, and in all forms of advertising, for example. Try not to be afraid of using it – think of it in just the same way as you think of the other language you know.

If you get a chance, look at any transcripts you can find of natural spoken English, and highlight some of the features you come across in this book: 'vague' language such as *loads of* and *stuff*; the adverbs *actually*, *anyway* and *then*; 'marker' words like *you see*, *I mean* and *right*.

Listen to the CD from time to time, not just as you work with the book, but also on its own, repeating and getting familiar with the language.

To the teacher

This book is primarily intended for self-study, but there is plenty of material for students to work together on in class as well. Exercises from the book might also be set for homework. The contents section will help you to plan activities related to whatever other material you are using. Sometimes the 'extension' activities at the end of units can be adapted for class use.

Once your students are generally aware of spoken grammar, you can, for example, set up simple oral activities such as students circulating and asking each other everyday questions like *Did you have a good weekend?*, *What sort of things do you do in your spare time?* and *What kind of food do you like?* As students talk, or later on in your 'round-up', you can 'feed in' some of the spoken grammar features they have come across in this book.

1 SHORT QUESTIONS FOR EVERYDAY CONVERSATIONS

About the language

> More tea?   Yes, please. Half a cup is fine, though.
>
> In conversation, we ask questions all the time. But quite often we only use the endings of questions, or we use very short questions with *about* or with prepositions. In this unit, we look at these ways of making short questions.

▶ For more short questions, see also Unit 16, page 69.

1 Using the endings of questions

<u>Underline</u> the two short questions in the dialogue below, and decide what the 'full' or longer questions would be. Check your answers on page 9.

Alice: It's nice here, isn't it?
Tim: Very pleasant, yes. More coffee?
Alice: No thanks. Why don't you finish it off?
Tim: Thanks. By the way, Elaine rang me from London about twenty minutes ago.
Alice: I thought she might get in touch. Any news?
Tim: Yes, she wants us to stay in Italy for another few days to make some more contacts.

With questions that end in the following ways, we often use the last part of the question only:
more + food or drink
any + *news*, *messages*, *phone calls*, *e-mails*, *letters*, etc.
any + *luck*, *chance*

The examples below show which parts of the sentence can be left out:

1 **A: More cake?** (~~Would you like some~~ more cake?)
   B: No, thanks. I've had two pieces already.
   A: Well, if you're sure.

2 **A:** Hi, Steve. I'm back. **Any calls for me?** (~~Have there been~~ any calls for me?)
   B: No, Di. It's been very quiet.

3 **A:** I've been looking for a new job.
   B: Oh. **Any luck?** (~~Have you had~~ any luck?)
   A: Not so far, I'm afraid.

4 **A: Any chance of a lift into town?** (~~Is there~~ any chance of a lift into town?)
   B: Of course. I'll be leaving in about ten minutes.

▶ Practice: Exercises 1, 2, 5 and 6 pages 10–11.
▶ For more information on words we don't need to use, see Unit 10, page 44.

About the language

2 Using *about* in short questions

Look at the short questions in bold in the dialogues below. What do they mean? If you had to express them in another way, what would you say? Check your answers below.

1 **A:** I'm ready to go home now. **What about you?**
  B: No, I'm not tired yet.

2 **A:** I'm starving. **How about some pasta?**
  B: Sounds great. There's a restaurant on Green Street.

If you want to keep a conversation going, one of the most useful short questions is *What about you?* We use it to find out about someone else, after expressing our own opinion/talking about ourselves:

A: I think I need some get some fresh air. **What about you?**
B: Sounds like a good idea. Where shall we go?

And you? means the same as *What about you?* but it's a little more formal. We sometimes use it in a reply to the question *How are you?*:

A: How are you?
B: I'm okay, thanks. **And you?**
A: I'm fine, thanks.

We also use *How about ...?* and sometimes *What about ...?* to make suggestions about things like food, drink and leisure activities:

A: We've twenty minutes before the meeting. **How about a coffee?**
B: Good idea.

▶ **Practice: Exercises 2, 3, 5 and 6 pages 10–11.**

3 Short questions with prepositions

To continue a conversation about leisure activities, we often use five short questions with prepositions to ask for information:

1 *What's on?* = What's happening at the moment on TV/at the cinema, etc.?
2 *What's it about?* = What's the subject of the film/book, etc.?
3 *When's/What time's it on?* = What time does it start?
4 *Who's in it?* = Who are the actors in the film/TV programme, etc.?
5 *Who's it by?* = Who wrote/directed/sang it?

Another very common short question with a preposition is *What's up?* It usually means *What's wrong?/What's the matter?*

A: You look worried. **What's up?**
B: I can't find my wallet anywhere.

▶ **Practice: Exercises 4, 5 and 6 pages 10–11.**

Answers

1 More coffee? Would you like some more coffee?   Any news? Did she give you any news?

2 1 Do you feel the same?   2 Shall we have some pasta?

1 SHORT QUESTIONS FOR EVERYDAY CONVERSATIONS

Practice

> To make sure you sound interested and polite, your intonation should rise at the end of these short questions.

1a Make these questions shorter.

1. Would you like some more coffee? _More coffee?_
2. Have there been any messages? _____
3. Do you want some more orange juice? _____
4. Has there been any news? _____
5. Have we had any phone calls? _____
6. Would you like some more sugar? _____

b Listen to check your answers. Which words are stressed? Listen again and <u>underline</u> the stressed words.

2 Where possible, cross out the questions in the conversation and write shorter versions.

Sue: That was so delicious! Thanks Phil.
Phil: No problem. ~~Would you like some more spaghetti?~~ _More spaghetti?_
Sue: I don't think I can, I'm completely full.
Phil: Have you had enough to eat, Jan?
Jan: I'll have a bit more please, if nobody else wants it.
Phil: Of course, here, help yourself. I'm going to make some coffee. Would you like some coffee too?
Sue: Yeah, that'd be good, thanks.
Jan: Is there any chance I could have a cold drink please?
Phil: Sure. Would you like some coke or juice?
Jan: Coke please.
Phil: Would you like something cold too, Sue?
Sue: No, just coffee's fine, thanks.

3a Add a question or complete the questions in the dialogues.

1. **A:** I think I've had enough to eat. _How about you?_
   B: Actually, I still have room for pudding!
2. **A:** How are you?
   B: I'm fine, thanks. _____?
3. **A:** _____ a game of tennis tomorrow?
   B: That sounds fun. Yeah, why not?
4. **A:** I haven't bought my outfit for the wedding yet and it's only three weeks away. _____?
   B: No, me neither!
5. **A:** _____ a cup of coffee?
   B: Now? It's a bit too late for me, I'm afraid. I'll never be able to sleep.
6. **A:** We still haven't decided where we're going on Saturday, have we?
   B: Oh yeah, well, _____ seeing that new Ken Loach film?

b Listen to check your answers. Notice how the word *about* is always in its weak form. Practise the dialogues, paying particular attention to the weak forms.

4 Match the questions 1–5 with the meanings a–e.

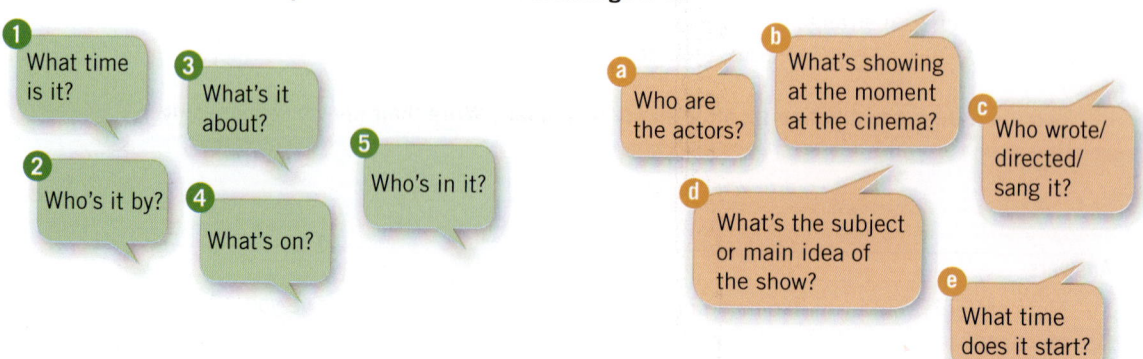

1. What time is it?
2. Who's it by?
3. What's it about?
4. What's on?
5. Who's in it?

a. Who are the actors?
b. What's showing at the moment at the cinema?
c. Who wrote/directed/sang it?
d. What's the subject or main idea of the show?
e. What time does it start?

10

PRACTICE

5a Choose suitable questions from Exercise 4 to complete the dialogue.

Isla: So, what do you fancy doing tonight?
Josh: I'm not sure. How about a film or something?
Isla: That could be good. ¹_____
Josh: Actually, there's a new thriller out this week.
Isla: Oh, okay. ²_____?
Josh: Martin Scorsese. Do you like his stuff?
Isla: I don't really know his films. ³_____
Josh: A murder – it's supposed to be really gripping.
Isla: Well, maybe. ⁴_____
Josh: Nobody famous. They're all unknown actors.
Isla: Okay, let's give it a go. ⁵_____
Josh: Eight-thirty at the Odeon. Perhaps we could get something to eat first?
Isla: Great. Let's go!

b Listen to check your answers. Then listen again and underline the words that are stressed.

6 Complete the MSN messages with the phrases in the box.

Any luck • What's on • What about you • What's up • How about • ~~Any news~~

Hi T
¹ _Any news?_ ? I haven't seen you in college recently. ²_____? You're not ill, are you? The last time we spoke you were looking for a part-time job ³_____? Anyway, let's get together. How about a drink one night? Maybe we could try and catch a film afterwards.
X

Hi K
Good to hear from you. I'm okay, but my granddad died and I went up to Scotland for the funeral. But I did get a job, in that Chinese restaurant in George Street.
⁴_____? You were looking for something part-time, too, weren't you? Sure, let's meet up for a drink. Monday evening's good for me. ⁵_____ a drink at our usual place at 7? Catching a film sounds great.⁶_____ , anything good?

Extension

1 Write messages for situations 1–3.

1 to a flatmate, asking about shopping needed
2 to a friend, to arrange lunch
3 to a colleague, asking about news at work while you've been away

2 Two old friends are meeting up after a long time apart. Write their conversation, using the phrases below. Record your dialogue, paying attention to stress and intonation.

What about you?   Any news about ...?   Any chance of ...?   How about ...?
When's it on?

11

2 COMMON STRUCTURES WITH *KNOW* AND *THINK*

About the language

> I don't know what to do.   Well, I don't think you should do anything for the moment.

Some short structures or word patterns of words are used again and again in spoken English as a 'springboard' for our sentences. In this unit, we look at four of these structures, and the kind of language that follows them.

1 *I don't know…*

(05) Underline the word that comes after *know* in the dialogues. Then listen and repeat, paying attention to the intonation.

> 1 A: I don't know what to do today.
> B: Why don't we have a game of tennis?
>
> 2 A: I don't know when Pete is arriving. Do you?
> B: Some time around six, I think.
>
> 3 A: I don't know where I've left my glasses.
> B: Have you tried looking in the bedroom?

springboard

One of the most frequent structures in spoken English is *I don't know + what/when/where/which/who/why/how …*

Here are some examples:

> 1 Both of the jumpers look great to me, so **I don't know which** one to buy.
> 2 I normally go by car. **I don't know how** to get there by train.

Sometimes we don't finish the sentence:

> 1 I spoke to one of your colleagues on the phone, but **I don't know who.** ~~I spoke to.~~
> 2 A: Sue left quite early, didn't she?
> B: Yes. **I don't know why.**

We also use *I don't know + if/whether*:

> **I don't know whether** she'll bring the tickets with her.

▶ Practice: Exercises 1, 3 and 5 pages 14–15.
▶ For more information on using *you know*, see Unit 5: **Send signals with …** page 24.

2 *I don't think (that) …*

In the sentences below, what is the difference in tone between the first and second sentence of each pair? Check your answers on page 13.

> 1a You look tired. I don't think we should go out tonight.
> b You look tired. We shouldn't go out tonight.
>
> 2a Tom is trying to repair my computer, but I don't think he knows what he's doing.
> b Tom is trying to repair my computer, but he doesn't know what he's doing.

If you listen to English people talking, you'll soon notice how often they use this structure to start a sentence: *I don't think (that) + I/you/he/she/it/we/they…*

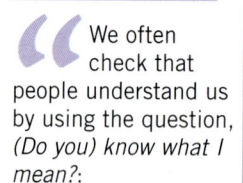

> " We often check that people understand us by using the question, *(Do you) know what I mean?*:
>
> *I'm feeling worried and excited at the same time – **know what I mean?***

ABOUT THE LANGUAGE

We can use this structure when we're simply not sure about something. But just as often, we use it because it allows us to express a view without sounding too direct. Here are three examples:

1 I **don't think** I can do any more work on this essay tonight. I'll try to finish it tomorrow.
2 You're welcome to borrow it, but **I don't think it's** the kind of book you'll enjoy.
3 Holly's been offered a great job, but **I don't think she** really wants to go to America.

▶ Practice: Exercise 2 page 14.

3 I think (that) …, I thought (that) …

What kind of structures follow the phrase *I think*? What is different about the structure in dialogue 3? Check your answers below.

1 **A:** Do you know where the lecture is?
   B: Yes, **I think it**'s in Room 352.
2 **A:** Who paid for the hotel?
   B: I'm not sure. **I think it was** Jaci.
3 **A:** Have a break. You look tired.
   B: Yes, **I think I might.**
4 **I think you** should take a look on the internet. You could find something cheaper.

We also use *I was thinking of…*:

A: **I was thinking** of having a bath.
B: Good idea. It will help you relax.

I thought (that) + you/he/she/it/that/they + was/were…

1 **A:** I thought you were having a day off.
   B: No. I'm just starting late. I have a meeting at eleven.
2 **A:** How was your exam?
   B: I thought that it was quite easy, actually.

I thought (that) + I would/you said …

1 **I thought I would** visit my mother this weekend. I haven't seen her since Christmas.
2 **A:** **I thought you said** you were dieting!
   B: I am, but I'm starting next week.

▶ Practice: Exercises 3, 4 and 5 pages 14–15.

> ❝ We sometimes start sentences with *I thought to myself*:
> **A:** Have you been to the gym?
> **B:** No. **I thought to myself**, 'It's a nice evening. I'll have a walk.'
>
> **I thought to myself**, 'I'll have a nice cup of tea' – but there wasn't any milk!

Answers

2 In each case, the first sentence is 'softer' or less direct.
3 *I think* is followed by *it's/it was/I might/you should*. In dialogue 3, speaker B stops after *might* (i.e. the phrase *have a break* does not have to be added).

2 COMMON STRUCTURES WITH *KNOW* AND *THINK*

Practice

1a Complete the sentences with *I don't know + what/where/when/which/who/why/how*.

1 I was talking to one of your colleagues, but <u>I don't know who</u> she is.
2 _____ the conference room is – is it on the first floor?
3 Sheila's got problems and wants me to help her, but _____ to help her.
4 The twins look so similar, _____ one is Pete!
5 _____ the bank is closed, do you? Is it a public holiday?
6 **A:** Have you got the dates for the festival?
  B: No, _____ it is.
7 David seems to have disappeared off the face of the earth! _____ he's doing. Is he travelling perhaps?
8 The receptionist said the toilets were on this floor, but _____ they are.

> *Disappeared off the face of the earth* means 'hasn't been seen for a long time'.

b Which two sentences do not need any more information after the gap?

2 Match the statements/questions 1–8 with the responses a–h.

1 Did you talk to the man from NASA? *g*
2 It's getting really late.
3 Can we go on the rollercoaster ride again?
4 I don't think you should spend any more on books.
5 Jonty and Mo are splitting up. Should I talk to Mo?
6 Let's plan a big surprise party for Susie!
7 Shall we spend all our money on a safari?
8 I don't think Jack will come to Peru with us.

a No, Let's not. I don't think she'll like it.
b Why not? He seemed enthusiastic last week.
c I don't think I could do it again: I feel sick!
d I know. I don't think they'll be coming now.
e No, I don't think it's a good idea; we should just go to Spain.
f No. I don't think we should interfere.
g ~~Yes. I don't think he's really an astronaut.~~
h No, you're right. It's getting really expensive.

3 Complete the sentences with the phrases in the box.

I think it's • I think it was (x2) • I don't know why • I think I might •
I think you should • I was thinking of • I don't know whether
---

> *To have your money's worth out of something* means 'to get the maximum value'.

1 **A:** Who was that on the phone?
  B: Not sure; _____ someone from Accounts.
2 _____ get a new laptop. You've had your money's worth out of this one!
3 Mimi's coming but _____ she'll bring her husband with her.
4 **A:** Have you seen my camera anywhere?
  B: Yes, _____ on the table by the door.
5 **A:** _____ go to bed early.
  B: That's a good idea; you look a bit tired.
6 _____ renting a cottage for the summer. If I did, would you come and stay?
7 **A:** Who took the minutes for the staff meeting I missed?
  B: I wasn't there either, but _____ Matt.
8 _____ you're laughing. It isn't funny.

14

PRACTICE

4a Listen and underline the stressed syllables.

1. **A:** I thought she was a bit rude to you.
   B: It's okay, I'm used to it!
2. **A:** Oh, what are you doing here? I thought you were going to Trish's party.
   B: No, I didn't feel like it.
3. I thought the audience looked really bored during Roger's speech.
4. Mexico? I thought they were emigrating to the United States!
5. I thought I would look for a new dress in the sales.
6. Jane! I thought you said you weren't coming!

b Listen again and repeat, focusing on stress and intonation.

c Which sentence/s show:

1 intention?   2 surprise?   3 personal belief or opinion?

5 Read the conversation between Nuala and her tutor, Becky. It contains eight grammatical mistakes. Find the mistakes and correct them. The first one has been done for you.

don't think

Becky: Well, Nuala, this is a very good essay, so I'm not thinking you should worry about getting a bad grade. Actually, I am think you will probably get a 2:1 or even a First.
Nuala: Oh wow, I'm so pleased. I really love Dublin architecture, but I wasn't sure if I could actually say anything worthwhile about it. Becky, while I'm here, can I ask you about my next assignment?
Becky: Sure, go ahead.
Nuala: Well, I not know if you'll agree with this, but I did thought of taking a look at some modern Irish sculpture next – Barry Flanagan's rabbits. I have thought I would try to compare his work with other twentieth-century animal sculptors.
Becky: That's really very interesting, but I thought you say you wanted to specialise in Dublin architecture. That's what you wrote in your proposal.
Nuala: I know, but I think I will like to change that, if it's not too late.
Becky: Well, I didn't know what the exam board will say about this, but we can ask for their advice.
Nuala: Thanks ever so much.

Extension

Look at the situations 1–5. Write a short dialogue for each, using some of the language you have practised in this unit. Read the dialogues aloud.

1. You are trying to find Liverpool Lime Street railway station, so you ask a passer-by for help. The passer-by is not sure either, but you try to work it out together.
2. You are with your friend, Harry. You are talking about another friend, Jasmine, who you believe is having relationship problems.
3. You are discussing your holiday plans with a colleague, but you aren't sure yet where or when you are going. Your colleague listens and tries to give advice.
4. You and your boyfriend/girlfriend are in a restaurant and discussing the food.
5. You and your flatmates are planning a quiet night in the flat tonight. Discuss what you are going to do.

3 MODIFY MEANING WITH *ACTUALLY, REALLY, OF COURSE*, ETC.

About the language

> **Anyway**, the train didn't stop.   Oh dear. Were you late, **then**?
>
> In conversation we often do more than simply express a basic meaning. Sometimes, for example, we also show our 'attitude' to what we're saying (e.g. surprise). Sometimes we 'soften' our language, especially if we have a different opinion, or want someone to do something for us. The adverbs in this unit are very useful for these situations.

1 *Actually, really, of course*

Read dialogues 1 and 2 below. What are the meanings of the words in bold? Think how the conversation might sound different if they weren't there. Check your answers on page 17.

> 1 A: Are you **actually** going out in that rain?
>   B: **Of course**. I've got to get to work, haven't I?
>
> 2 A: I shouldn't have criticised you like that in front of everyone. I'm sorry.
>   B: It's alright, **really**. I don't mind. I'd rather people said what they thought.

Actually, *really* and *of course* emphasise that something is true, but we use them in different ways. We normally use *actually* when there is something surprising about the thing we are saying/ or doing:

> These vegetarian burgers **actually** taste quite nice.

At the beginning of a sentence, *actually* can suggest that we're about to talk about something specific:

> A: You could have phoned me, you know.
> B: **Actually**, I need to speak to you face to face.

We also use *actually* as a softening word, when we are saying sorry, for example:

> I forgot to tell you about the party, **actually**.

It is also used to express a slightly different point of view:

> I know he's loud but I like him, **actually**.

As well as using *really* before some words to make them stronger (*I **really** love Italian food.*), we can use it to express surprise:

> A: He doesn't use a mobile phone, you know.
> B: **Really**? How does he keep in touch with people?

🔊(07) **Listen to the intonation in the dialogues 1–3. Notice how *really* can be a softening word. Listen again and repeat, paying attention to intonation.**

> 1 A: I'm sorry I shouted.
>   B: Don't worry. It's okay, **really**.
>
> 2 A: Do you want to come?
>   B: **Not really**. (= no)
>
> 3 A: You didn't like him, did you?
>   B: No, **not really**.

The phrase *of course* suggests that something is obvious:

> 1 It's a lovely flat but it's expensive, **of course**.
> 2 **Of course** the sea was still very cold in May.

ABOUT THE LANGUAGE

It can also just mean *yes*:

A: Can I leave my coat there? **B:** **Of course**.

▶ Practice: Exercises 1, 2, 3, 4 and 6 pages 18–19.

2 *Anyway, then, though*

Listen to a conversation just before a business meeting. Which one of the words in bold signals a change in the direction of the conversation? Check your answers below.

Neera: Katie! Good to see you. You got here okay, **then**?
Katie: Yes. The traffic was a bit slow. Mustn't complain, **though**. It's a lovely place, isn't it?
Neera: Really interesting, yes. (*Looking at her watch*) **Anyway**, I suppose we'd better get to the meeting.

Anyway, *then* and *though* are 'linking' adverbs. *Anyway* means 'now it's time for me to say something more important':

… so we walked along one street after another, getting more and more lost! **Anyway**, we got there in the end and had a great time.

We often use it at the end of stories, or when it's time to leave, or start something:

1 **Anyway**, we'd better be getting home now.
2 **Anyway**, if everyone is here, shall we start?

We also use *anyway* at the end of sentences, where it means something like 'despite':

The film was an hour too long, but I enjoyed it **anyway**. (despite the length)

Then can mean 'at that time' (*I worked for a bank* ***then***.) or 'next' (*… and **then** we moved to Paris.*) But often in spoken English, it means something like 'in that case':

A: We only stayed at her party for half an hour. **B:** You didn't enjoy it, **then**?

And we often use *so* with *then*:

A: I never eat Indian food. **B:** **So** you don't like spicy things, **then**?

Finally, we sometimes put *though* at the end of a sentence in spoken English, where it means something like 'however':

I'm enjoying the job. It's hard work, **though**.

▶ Practice: Exercise 5 page 19.

> *Right then*, and *Okay then*, are used in a similar way to *anyway*. But *Now then*, is a phrase we also use to 'calm' people:
> **Now then**, I'm sure we can work this out.

3 *Just*

Just has a number of meanings such as 'very recently' (*I've **just** finished.*), 'exactly' (*That's **just** what I wanted!*) and 'only' (*There's **just** one left.*). But there is another meaning, very common in spoken English, that combines the idea of 'only' with a softening effect:

1 I **just** want to explain to you why I left early last night. (Please listen for a moment.)
2 Can you **just** turn the volume down, please? (I'm not asking very much.)

▶ Practice: Exercise 6 page 19.

> If you're in a shop and you don't want to buy something immediately, say to the assistant: *I'm just looking, thanks.*

Answers

1 *Actually* expresses surprise; *of course* means 'it's obvious'; *really* emphasises the fact that the speaker is alright, and therefore 'softens' the response.
2 Anyway

17

3 MODIFY MEANING WITH ACTUALLY, REALLY, OF COURSE, ETC.

Practice

> Intonation is very important when using these modifiers. If the speaker's voice goes up during the utterance ↗, they sound much more polite and friendly. If the intonation goes down ↘, they sound impolite or uninterested

1 Listen to the dialogues and decide if speaker B is being friendly (F) or unfriendly (U).

1. **A:** I'm sorry, I didn't mean to upset you.
   B: It's okay, really.
2. **A:** Is it okay to come in?
   B: Of course.
3. **A:** She's going to be thirty this year.
   B: Really? I thought she was much older than that.
4. **A:** Is he coming home tonight?
   B: Of course, why did you ask?
5. **A:** Did you like the film?
   B: Not really.
6. **A:** Where is John?
   B: He's late again, of course.

2a Cross out the incorrect *really* in each sentence.

1. I really hate ~~really~~ tomatoes!
2. The really weather in Belgium is really hot at the moment.
3. **A:** Waiter! My food's too spicy!
   B: Sshh! Really do you really want to send it back to the kitchen?
4. **A:** Would you like a piece of cake?
   B: Not really; it will spoil really my diet.
5. **A:** I shouldn't pay this much for a dress.
   B: Well, it's not that really expensive, really.
6. **A:** I don't like dogs.
   B: Really? Where you really bitten by one or something?
7. **A:** Sorry, I must have upset you.
   B: Really no, you didn't really.
8. **A:** I can't stand her!
   B: Oh, come on, do really you really mean that?

b Listen to check your answers. Then listen and repeat, paying particular attention to the stress and intonation in each sentence.

3 <u>Underline</u> the correct word/phrase to complete the sentences.

1. **A:** Are those new shoes you bought okay to wear?
   B: Yes, they're *actually/of course* very comfortable.
2. **A:** Where did you go this afternoon?
   B: Well, I went for a walk after we had that argument, *really/actually*. I should have told you.
3. **A:** Did you like Peter's new girlfriend?
   B: *Really./Of course.* I thought she was very nice.
4. **A:** I've got all the ingredients for the pudding.
   B: *Oh, actually?/Oh, really?* Oh no, I'm sorry, I've decided to serve cheese and biscuits instead.
5. **A:** Is it okay if I use your bathroom?
   B: Oh, *really./of course.* It's upstairs on the right.
6. **A:** They say that Michael Jackson's not dead.
   B: Why, has anyone *of course/actually* seen him?

18

PRACTICE

4 Complete the phone conversation with *actually*, *really* or *of course*.

Rowan: I'd ¹_____ love to go right up north to the Highlands when we're in Scotland, but I'm not sure if we've got time.

Michelle: Well … it would be easy to cut short our stay in Edinburgh, ²_____, and leave on Thursday.

Rowan: ³_____, I meant to tell you this sooner, but we have to stay in Edinburgh till the Saturday because I bought a ticket for the match in the afternoon.

Michelle: The match! Oh, ⁴_____, I should have known you'd do that! ⁵_____, it's not a problem because …

Rowan: ⁶_____? I thought you'd be angry!

Michelle: ⁷_____ not, we're on holiday. Anyway, I thought I might meet Toby if he's around. I haven't seen him for ages, and it'd be a ⁸_____ great opportunity to catch up.

Rowan: What, Toby, your ex? So, while I'm watching the football, you'll be meeting your ex-boyfriend!

Michelle: Good, well, that's settled then.

> It's important to stress the modifying words and phrases to get your message across.

5 Complete the sentences with *anyway*, *then*, or *though*.

1 It rained all the way through my camping weekend, but I enjoyed it _____.

2 **A:** I've bought a car!
   B: So you'll be able to drive me around _____!

3 **A:** I don't want to go out with Hugh tonight.
   B: You promised him _____.

4 **A:** I wish we could see more of our friends.
   B: I know, but we live such a long way away now _____.

5 **A:** I didn't have any money to buy petrol with.
   B: How did you fill your tank, _____?

6 What a great party, thanks! I've met so many interesting people. _____, I should be getting home now. It's really late.

7 He's selfish and immature. I love him _____.

8 … so first the cat got stuck up the tree, and then so did the fire fighter who came to rescue him! _____, we got everyone down in the end.

6 Add the word *actually*, *really* or *just* in an appropriate place in each sentence/dialogue.

1 **A:** Do you like swimming?
   B: No, not really.

2 Can you listen for a second while I explain why I didn't call you?

3 I know you think the music's awful, but I like it.

4 **A:** Sorry I took your last bit of money.
   B: I've already told you not to worry. It's okay.

5 I know you're busy, but couldn't you come for the beginning of the party?

6 **A:** How's Sue getting on with the job-hunting?
   B: She's got an interview this afternoon.

7 **A:** Is she your girlfriend?
   B: No, we're flatmates.

8 **A:** Shall we watch the documentary, or do you want to see that new quiz show?
   B: I don't mind what we watch.

Extension

Write down five facts about yourself that others might find surprising. Now, imagine you're telling somebody. Make sentences using *actually*. Record your sentences, paying particular attention to stress and intonation.

4 IMPROVE YOUR NAMING SKILLS

About the language

> Where are we eating, **guys**? I'm not sure, **Mike**. They say the Italian place is good.
>
> There are three main ways of addressing people: by first name; by title (e.g. *Mr Smith*); and by general words such as *guys*. Whatever you use, you need to take care. A general guide is to listen to what is acceptable in your social circle, or to ask a question like: *Can I call you Alison?* If you use a title such as *Mr Brown*, you may find that the person says something like, *Please call me Brian*.

1 First names

Think about how you use first names in your country. What are the different purposes for using them? Do you normally place them at the beginning, middle or end of a sentence?

We use first names or nicknames at the beginning of sentences to get people's attention:

1 **Ade**, dinner's ready!
2 Hey **Jo**! We're over here!
3 (*on the phone*) **Mike**, are you still there?
4 (*passing a bowl of rice across the table*) **Chris**? (↗)

The most common position for a first name, however, is actually the end of a sentence. There are three main purposes.

1 to be friendly:

> It's a lovely day, isn't it, **Louis**?

2 to 'identify' someone in a group:

> A: Shall we meet at the cinema, **Jay**?
> B: Alright, **Meg**. Is that okay with you, **Pete**?

3 as a 'softener' because we're interrupting someone, for example, or because they're unhappy:

1 Wait a moment, **Barry**. Are you sure you're right?
2 Try not to worry about it right now, **Holly**.

Using a first name in the middle of a sentence is more unusual, but again softening is often the purpose. In this example, the speaker decides to make a request less direct:

> Could I possibly look something up, **Dave**, on your computer?

▶ Practice: Exercise 1 and 6 pages 22–23.

2 Titles

Before you read the next two sections, think about where you might hear the following terms: *mate, officer, guys, madam, dear*. Then check your answers on page 21.

In formal situations, the titles *Mr*, *Mrs*, and *Miss* are used with the person's surname alone. There is a fourth, more recent term, *Ms*, pronounced /mɪz/, for a woman who may or may not be married. These words are hardly ever used on their own, except in a jokey or sometimes an angry manner. The titles *professor*, *doctor* and *officer* (for a police officer) are, however, occasionally used on their own. Here are some examples of all these:

1 (*at an interview*) **Mr Roberts**, could you come in now?
2 (*to a child*) Have you finished playing in the mud then, **miss**?
3 (*at the cinema*) Hey, **mister**! Do you know you're kicking the back of my seat?
4 Could I ask you to recommend a journal, **professor**?
5 (*to a policeman*) Is there something going on **officer**?

ABOUT THE LANGUAGE

The titles *sir* (for men) and *madam* (for women) are used by shopkeepers, waiters and officials, but not normally by people in general:

1 Can I show you some of the other perfumes, **madam**?
2 (*at an airport*) Could you open your bag, please, **sir**?

▶ Practice: Exercises 2 and 6 pages 22–23.

3 General words

When we are addressing a group of equals, a common term is *guys*, or sometimes *folks* (both originally American). These terms can be used for men and women:

Folks, are you ready to leave?

A group of women together may be called *girls* or *ladies*, and a group of men *boys*, *lads* or the upper-class *chaps* – but often just in a 'jokey' way:

1 Let's have a night out together then, **girls**!
2 We're going to be late for the game, **chaps**, aren't we?

The terms *everybody/everyone* and *children* are sometimes used by people in organising roles:

1 Could you leave quietly, please, **everyone**?
2 Children, please wipe your feet before you come in.

At formal situations such as weddings, we address audiences as *ladies and gentlemen*:

Ladies and gentlemen, I'd like to say what a pleasure it's been, knowing John all these years.

With all these plural terms, you need to make a careful judgment that they will be appropriate before using them.

In British English, the singular, very informal term *mate* is used, normally to address men, and *man* is sometimes used by younger people – to address men **and** women:

1 Have you got the time, **mate**?
2 Man, that was a tough essay.
3 What's up, **man**?

Americans use *buddy* for *mate*, and younger Americans say: *man, dude, bro'* (brother).

In UK shops and cafés, female servers sometimes address men and women as *dear* and *love* (*Here's your change, dear.*) and male servers sometimes use these terms (and also *darling*) for women – but all these expressions may be seen as rather old-fashioned, even sexist.

For people in a close relationship, all sorts of terms are possible. The most common positive ones you might hear are: *baby, darling, dear, honey, love, luvvie, sweetheart*:

1 Could you put the kettle on, **sweetheart**?
2 Darling, nothing is too much effort for you!

Among the negative terms (often prefixed by *you*) there are: *slowcoach, lazybones, idiot*:

1 Get up, you **lazybones**!
2 Hurry up, **slowcoach**!
3 You **idiot**, why didn't you ring me?

▶ Practice: Exercises 3, 4, 5 and 6 pages 22–23.

Answers

2 *mate*: very informal term used to address men; *officer*: used for a police officer; *guys*: used to address an informal group of equals; *madam*: used by staff in shops, hotels, etc., to address women; *dear*: sometimes used by shop assistants; or by people in close relationships.

4 IMPROVE YOUR NAMING SKILLS

Practice

1 Circle the best response, *a* or *b*.

1 Oh hi, Ade! How're you doing?
   a Fine thanks Cath. You?   b I'm doing the washing-up, Cath.
2 Dilys? Is that you?
   a Who's that?   b Yes, it's me! Why, do I sound strange?
3 Excuse me Hugh, I need a private word with Ute.
   a Sure, no problem. I'll go and get some fresh air.
   b What are you going to say to her?
4 What would you like to drink, Rosa?
   a I'd like to drink something.   b Oh, a glass of diet coke, please.
5 Could I use your phone please, Kwab?
   a No.   b Of course, here you are.
6 Hang on a minute, Sigita, what's wrong?
   a Oh, I've just had some bad news.   b I'm not telling you.
7 Suki, can you come to my office please?
   a I don't think so!   b Of course, but can I just finish this e-mail?
8 Oh Stew, that's wonderful news!
   a Yeah, it's really great, isn't it?   b It's none of your business!

2a Listen to the titles 1–9 and repeat. For each syllable do you hear the 'full' vowel sound or the 'weak' schwa /ə/ sound?

1 Mr   _full_   _weak_
2 Mrs _____   _____
3 Miss _____
4 Ms   _____
5 Professor _____ _____ _____
6 Madam _____ _____
7 Sir _____
8 Officer _____ _____ _____
9 Doctor _____ _____

> *Ms* is used as a title by a lot of women nowadays, who do not feel comfortable being addressed as *Miss* or *Mrs*, as these both suggest a marital status. As with *Mr*, *Ms* keeps your marital status private.

b Choose a suitable title for the following people.

1 a middle-aged woman: you don't know if she's married
2 somebody with a PhD qualification
3 a policeman whose name you don't know
4 a man over the age of eighteen
5 a young girl

3 Underline the correct alternative to complete the sentences.

1 (*two families meeting in the park*) Hey! Long time no see! How are you *guys/ladies and gentlemen*?
2 (*in a café*) Here's your change, *man/dear*.
3 (*parent*) Come on *kids/man*, go and wash your hands for dinner!
4 (*in an office*) Hey, *guys/ladies and gentlemen*, you'll never believe who I've just seen!
5 (*at the theatre*) *Everyone/Ladies and gentlemen*, please take your seats, tonight's performance will begin in two minutes.
6 (*fire marshal in a public building*) Could *everyone/folks* please leave the building quickly and assemble in the square!

PRACTICE

4a Complete the dialogues with a suitable title.

1. **A:** Can I take your name please?
   B: Yes, it's Pippa Oades, that's O-A-D-E-S.
   A: _____ Oades?
   B: No, it's _____ , actually!

2. **A:** (*waiter speaking to woman*) Can I take your coat, _____?
   B: Oh, thank you.

3. **A:** (*policeman to a man caught speeding*) Would you step out of the car please, _____?
   B: Certainly, _____. Is there anything wrong?

4. **A:** (*at the doctor's surgery*) How can I help you?
   B: I've had this cough, _____, for about a month.

5. **A:** (*pedestrian to a male cyclist at a crossing*) Hey _____, watch where you're going, you nearly knocked me over!
   B: Oh sorry, _____ but you just stepped out in front of me!

6. **A:** (*in a college corridor*) Can I give you this essay now, _____?
   B: Well, it's rather late. The deadline was Friday.

b Listen to check your answers. Then listen and repeat, paying attention to stress and intonation.

5 Match 1–6 with a–f to make sentences.

1. Put a coat on
2. What time do you call this, you
3. You silly fool! You've
4. Get a move
5. Oh baby, it's been
6. Oh hello, darling! What

a. a lovely surprise to see you here at work.
b. ages! I've missed you so much!
c. sweetheart, it's cold outside.
d. idiot! You could have rung me earlier.
e. on, slowcoach. We're going to be late.
f. lost your phone again, haven't you?

6 Some friends are having a meal in a restaurant. Complete their conversation with the phrases in the box.

Ladies and gentlemen • having starters, folks • Hey guys • Come on, Em love • are we having, everyone • Certainly, sir • you idiot • Take it easy, man

Alex: ¹_____, shall we just go ahead and order without Emily? We've been waiting ages!
Carlos: We had a bit of an argument, actually. But I'm sure she's on her way.
Billy: Well, let's get some drinks at least. Come on, what ²_____?
Alex: Have we decided whether we're ³_____?
Carlos: Of course we are. It's included in the price ⁴_____!
Billy: Hey! ⁵_____.
Carlos: Sorry, I was only joking. Anyway boys, here comes Emily.
Emily: Oh, I'm so sorry everyone. Carlos, darling, have you forgiven me?
Carlos: Of course. ⁶_____, come and sit down. The waiter's coming.
Waiter: ⁷_____, are you ready to order?
Carlos: Can we just get two bottles of your house white wine to start with please? We need a bit more time to decide on food I think.
Waiter: ⁸_____. I'll get your drinks …

Extension

Answer the questions about your language.

1. How do you address strangers? Does it depend on age/gender/job?
2. Is it considered polite or rude to assume a woman is married or unmarried?
3. Do you have special titles for police? Other people in authority?
4. Do you have friendly ways of 'insulting' people (like *you idiot* in English)?

23

5 SEND SIGNALS WITH *I MEAN, YOU SEE, YOU KNOW*, ETC.

About the language

> *Right*, shall we have a break? *I mean*, we can't work all day, can we?
>
> Sometimes, in conversation, we use a word or short phrase to 'signal' the type of thing we're about to say (or we've just said). It's a bit like a driver signalling that their car is going to turn left or right. In this unit, we study the key 'signalling' expressions.

1 *I mean, you see, you know*

Before you look at the examples below, what general idea do you think the phrases *I mean*, *you see* and *you know* share? Check your answers on page 25.

I mean means something like 'I'm about to explain myself more clearly/fully':

> There's no need to hurry – **I mean**, it's only a ten-minute walk.

Sometimes, it suggests that we want to correct ourselves:

> I got a bit lost. **I mean**, not 'lost' but I forgot how long the road was.

You see is slightly different. It means something like 'this is the reason':

> I'm going to invite him for the weekend. **You see**, we really need a chance to talk.

You know (often pronounced *y'know*) suggests that the listener probably already knows what the speaker is talking about:

> … that restaurant, **you know**, the one with those big tables that you share.

You see and *you know* can also signal 'backwards' to something we've already said:

1 We'll have to book. It's become a very popular restaurant, **you know**.
2 I'll have to find another flat. This one's just too noisy, **you see**.

▶ Practice: Exercise 1 page 26.

2 *Right, well, so*

Right, a slightly stronger version of *okay*, sometimes just means 'I understand':

> A: … and the show starts at eight thirty.
> B: **Right**. Thanks.

But note that it is sometimes used ironically, when we don't really understand at all.

> A: … and then in the afternoon, we're going to climb all three mountains.
> B: **Right**. That sounds like fun.

> When *right* is used ironically, this is shown in the intonation as well as the context.

Right can also be quite a strong signal that we are at the beginning or end of a situation.

1 **Right**, we'd better start cooking.
2 **Right**, we're almost finished. If you could just sign here?

You normally need to be in control, or sharing control, to use *right* in this way. In a family car, for example, a parent could say *Right, shall we stop for lunch?*, but not a child.
Well can also signal a change, but it is often a signal of doubt, hesitation or contrast:

1 A: You didn't reply to my e-mail.
   B: **Well**, I didn't know what to say.
2 We must have walked all day, **well**, all afternoon.
3 A: I thought you liked spicy food.
   B: **Well**, I don't. I've told you before.

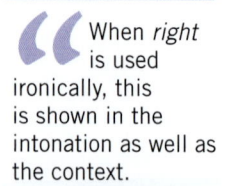

ABOUT THE LANGUAGE

So can also signal a change:

> **So**, I suppose it's time to get home. It's getting quite dark.

It can also be a request for clarification:

> **So**, what are you saying? Are you really suggesting you might give up college?

So can signal a return to an earlier subject of conversation:

> **So** what happened? Did you get your suitcases back in the end?

▶ **Practice: Exercises 2 and 3 pages 26–27.**

3 *Listen, look, hey*

Look at the examples below. What general idea do you think these three words share? Check your answers below.

> 1 **Hey**, look at the time! We'd better get going.
> 2 **Look**, you'll fail if you don't work harder.
> 3 **Listen**, we'll just make matters worse if we legalise drugs.

Listen and *look* mean 'please pay attention to what I am about to say':

> 1 **Listen**, if you don't vote, you can't criticise the government afterwards, can you?
> 2 I think you should finish your course but **look**, it's your decision in the end.

As with *right*, you can't really use these words in this way if you are in a 'junior' position – an applicant at a job interview, for example.

We use *hey* (often with a person's name) to catch a friend's attention:

> 1 **Hey** Rob! Come here! There's something I want to tell you.
> 2 **Hey**, look at that dog! It's huge.

Sometimes a person in authority will use it, often with children:

> **Hey**! Stop running about! This is a museum, not a playground.

It also has a kind of jokey use among adults:

> This is our third holiday this year – but **hey**, who's counting?

▶ **Practice: Exercise 4 page 27.**
▶ **For ways of using *well*, *listen*, *look* and *hey* to report speech, see Unit 14, page 60.**

4 Phrases with *say, speak, tell* and *talk*

Some signalling phrases actually use verbs that refer to the act of speaking:

> 1 **As I was saying**, she's going to be a great tennis player.
> 2 **Speaking of** Miriam, here she is! Hi, Miriam!
> 3 **I'll tell you what**, it's the best pizza I've ever eaten.
> 4 **Talking about** films, have you seen *The Last Day* yet?
> 5 **You mean to say** you don't like Picasso?

▶ **Practice: Exercise 5 page 27.**

Answers

1 They normally signal some kind of explanation (and all three give the speaker time to think).
3 They are all ways of attracting someone's attention.

5 SEND SIGNALS WITH *I MEAN, YOU SEE, YOU KNOW*, ETC.

> With *you know, I mean*, etc., remember not to stress the pronoun, but use the schwa (/ə/).

Practice

1 Match 1–8 with a–h to make sentences.

1 Did you see that film *I am Love*? It's really awful! I mean,
2 Let's go to that art gallery with all the Picassos in it. You know,
3 Hurry up, we're going to be late! I mean,
4 I'm sorry, you can't see the doctor today. You see,
5 I'm having lunch with my new colleague today. You know,
6 I'm not going to apply for that job – I mean
7 I didn't manage to get tickets for the music festival. You see,
8 What's the name of that really famous composer? You know,

a the one I told you about, she started on Monday.
b the one who wrote The Planets.
c his surgery ends at 5p.m.
d the acting is just so wooden.
e the lecture starts in ten minutes.
f the one near the station.
g you have to book straight away and I was too late!
h I'm just not qualified enough.

2a What is the meaning of *right* in sentences 1–6? Does it express understanding (U), signal the beginning of a situation (B) or the end of a situation (E)?

1 **A:** You need to take the first road on the left, and the cinema's on your right.
   B: *Right*, so first left, and it's on the right. Thanks.   U
2 *Right*, it's 8.30. We'd better get going or else we'll be late.
3 *Right*, I must go. I need to get up early in the morning. Thanks for a lovely evening.
4 *Right*, any other business? No? Great. I'd like to declare this meeting closed.
5 **A:** You need to go to 'insert' and scroll down to 'symbol' – it's there.
   B: *Right*, thanks, that's brilliant. No one's ever explained that before.
6 *Right*, I've done all my e-mails! What do you fancy doing now?

b Listen to check your answers. Then listen again and notice the different intonation between expressing understanding and signalling the beginning/ending of a situation.

3a <u>Underline</u> the correct alternative to complete the sentences.

1 He offered me the job! *Right/So*, what did you say?
2 **A:** Did you enjoy the exhibition?
   B: *Well/So* I'm not sure really, I don't understand modern art.
3 *Right/Well*, let's go. If we hurry, we'll catch the 7.30 showing of the film.
4 That was the best meal I've had for years – *right/well*, for a while.
5 **A:** This is his new number.   **B:** *Right./So*. Thanks.
6 **A:** But I'm not racist!
   B: *So/Well*, you sound it when you say things like that!

b Listen to check your answers. Then listen again, paying attention to the stressed words and the pauses. Practise reading the sentences aloud.

4a Match 1–8 with a–h to make sentences.

1 Listen, I'm cooking dinner at the moment,
2 Look, if you don't pay attention,
3 I wouldn't spend £500 on a dress, but hey,
4 Listen, I don't want to see you anymore –
5 Hey, there's that woman I was telling you about,
6 Look, I've had enough of this job –
7 He could be here any time, but look, your guess
8 Hey! Don't drop litter –

a we're finished!
b I quit!
c you won't know what to do.
d can I call you back later?
e there's a bin over there!
f it's not my money!
g over there by the window.
h is as good as mine.

PRACTICE

b Add a suitable follow-up sentence, to the sentences in exercise 4a on page 26.

1 I just don't love you anymore.
2 And I don't want to explain it all again.
3 Don't leave it for other people to pick up!
4 Are you in all evening?
5 I'll hand in my resignation tomorrow!
6 He's so unpredictable!
7 The one with the long hair.
8 It's yours!

5a Complete the dialogues with the phrases in the box, using capital letters where necessary.

as I was saying • speaking of • you mean to say • talking about • I'll tell you what

Javier: The match was great, Holland deserved to win, but I can't help feeling sorry for Uruguay.
Ashraf: Yeah, [1]_____ Uruguay, Tim got back from South America last week. He had a great time. [2]_____, he looks ten years younger.
Javier: Good for him. Anyway, [3]_____ shame about Uruguay eh?
Ashraf: Well, they did well to get to the semi-finals.

* * *

Selvi: I don't have a problem with fox-hunting. [4]_____ that kind of thing, I went to a bull-fight when I was in Madrid last week. It was amazing.
Brunella: [5]_____ you approve of blood sports? I can't believe it!
Selvi: Well, it's a way of controlling the numbers, especially foxes and things. Plus, it's tradition isn't it?
Brunella: Tradition? Come on, this is the twenty-first century!

b Listen and check your answers. Then listen again and repeat, paying attention to the stress and intonation.

Extension

1 **Look back at Exercise 3. What is the context for each sentence?**

2 **Write short dialogues using the opening sentences below.**

So, what happened? Did you get your money back?
I'm going to ask her to marry me. I mean, she's the one!
Listen, we've got to leave the country immediately!

3 **Record your dialogue. Think about the use of stress and pause.**

27

6 USE *SO* AND *DO* TO MAKE EFFECTIVE RESPONSES

About the language

> I've got to write up my report — So you said. But when will you actually do it?

So and ***do*** have many uses in English. They both play an important part, for example, in the business of 'connecting' bits of conversation together. In this unit, we focus on some ways of using these words as 'substitutes' – to refer to something that's already been said without actually repeating it – and to make emphatic responses.

1 *So* before verbs

Apart from responses like *So did I* and *So are we*, we also use *so* as a substitute before the verbs *say, tell, hear* and *believe*.

🔊 **b Listen and notice the intonation.**

1   **A:** Olivia and Jack are getting married.
    B: **So I heard.** It's great news.

2   **A:** House prices are going to fall, apparently.
    B: **So they say.** It's about time.

3   **A:** There are no trains today, I'm afraid.
    B: **So I believe.** Is there a bus instead?

So I understand and *So I gather* are also used, but more formally.

We can also use *so* in emphatic responses before *be, do, have* and modal verbs:

1   **A:** I'm going brown already.
    B: **So you are!** You'd better put some sun cream on.

2   **A:** I feel bad about losing my temper with Mark.
    B: **So you should.** But you apologised afterwards, didn't you?

▶ Practice: Exercise 1 page 30.

2 *So* after verbs

Before you read on, try to work out exactly what *so* stands for below. Check your answers on page 29.

   A: Did Greg get the job he applied for?
   B: Yes, I think **so**.

We use *so* after these verbs: *think, reckon, suppose, guess, say, tell, hope, expect, be afraid*:

1   **A:** We'll have to get a taxi.
    B: **I suppose so,** but it'll be expensive, won't it?

2   **A:** Jo will win the match, won't she?
    B: **I expect so.** She normally does.

3   **A:** It's going to pour.
    B: **I'm afraid so.** Have you got your umbrella?

I imagine/presume/assume so and *It appears/seems so* are used more formally:

   A: (*in a restaurant*) Do you mean that my credit card's been declined?
   B: **It appears so**, sir. Do you have another card?

> " We use *So you were saying* to tell someone that we know what they're talking about:
> **A:** I want to start learning Chinese.
> **B: So you were saying.** Have you found a course yet?

28

ABOUT THE LANGUAGE

With *suppose, guess, hope* and *be afraid*, replace *so* with *not* to form a negative:

> **A:** Look! Mike's going to sing.
> **B:** Really? I hope **not**.

With the other verbs, we prefer to use a regular negative form:

> No, **I don't think** so.

▶ Practice: Exercises 2 and 3 pages 30–31.

3 Do

Do can be a substitute in many types of response. Try using it to replace three consecutive words in the sentence below. Check your answer below.

> She listens to me more than you listen to me.

We can add *do* emphatically to short answers with *have*.

1 **A:** Have you e-mailed your boss?
  B: Yes, I **have done**, but she hasn't replied.

2 **A:** Has Lara come in?
  B: She **has done**, yes. She went upstairs.

We also use *do* after modal verbs:

1 **A:** You should ask for a pay rise.
  B: I would **do**, but the company's in trouble right now.

2 **A:** I ought to ring her now.
  B: You could **do**. It's late, though.

▶ Practice: Exercise 4 page 31.

4 Do it, do that

Do it and *do that* are very common in conversation. Often you can use either, but *do that* tends to be more emphatic and 'distant' from yourself:

1 **A:** Jack started shouting over lunch today.
  B: I know. He does **it/that** all the time these days.

2 **A:** They're going to charge entry to the museum in town.
  B: Really? They shouldn't **do that**.

Do this is possible, but less common. *Do so* is formal and normally used in writing or in something like a public announcement:

> We recommend a walk in the hills, but if you are planning to **do so**, make sure you have strong shoes and waterproof clothing.

▶ Practice: Exercise 4 page 31.

I don't like skating. I **did it** once, and I kept falling over.

Answers

2 Here *so* means 'he did get the job he applied for'.
3 She listens to me more than you do.

6 USE SO AND DO TO MAKE EFFECTIVE RESPONSES

Practice

1a Look at the pictures A–F and match them with the dialogues 1–6.

1 **A:** Work is very stressful at the moment.
  B: So I gather. Mimi rang me last night and told me.
2 **A:** I'm pregnant!
  B: So I see! Congratulations!
3 **A:** Is it true that 250 people have lost their jobs at the car factory?
  B: So I believe. I've been reading about it in the paper this morning.
4 **A:** I already told you I need to withdraw £1,000.
  B: So I understand, Mr Brown. But we can't give it to you until tomorrow.
5 **A:** Pam's coming over to stay for the summer!
  B: So Felix told me. I bumped into him on the High Street today.
6 **A:** Hey, Mark and Suza have split up.
  B: So I hear. She texted me earlier.

> *To dump someone* means to tell a boy/girlfriend that the relationship is finished.

b Listen and repeat, making sure you stress *So* and the verb.

c Add a suitable follow-up a–f to the dialogues 1–6 above.

a I'm so pleased for you both. Your families must be thrilled.
b We need proof of your identity.
c It'll be great to spend some time with her. She hasn't been back here for ages.
d It's really awful for all those families just before Christmas.
e He dumped her over the phone – she's absolutely heartbroken!
f It sounds like the new director is a bit of a nightmare.

30

PRACTICE

2 Underline the correct alternative to complete the dialogues.

1 **A:** Do you think we'll be able to get tickets for the show?
 B: Oh I *say/think* so. It's on for a while, so I'm sure they're still available.

2 **A:** Did Niall get that job he applied for?
 B: I *hope/I'm afraid* so. He really wanted it and he deserves a bit of good luck.

3 **A:** Is Nick definitely coming tonight?
 B: Well, he *told/said* so, but that was a fortnight ago and we didn't confirm anything.

4 **A:** Do we really have to go and visit your parents this weekend?
 B: I*'m afraid/hope* so. I know they can be difficult, but they love to see us.

5 **A:** Are you sure we're going the right way? It looks different on the map.
 B: I *think/say* so. I've been following your directions!

3 Complete the negative responses in the dialogues, using the verbs in brackets.

1 **A:** Is Sylvie cooking tonight?
 B: I *hope not*. She's a terrible cook! (hope)

2 **A:** Come on, let's have a cold drink before we set off home. It won't take long.
 B: Okay, _____ I could do with one – it's such a hot day! (suppose)

3 **A:** Are Katie and Hugh seeing each other?
 B: I _____. He's not her type. (think)

4 **A:** I don't think that dress is really formal enough for a wedding.
 B: I _____. Shall I wear the blue one instead? (guess)

5 **A:** Will there be any food at the party? I'm starving!
 B: I _____. I think we should grab a bite to eat on the way. (be afraid)

4 Complete the dialogue at the end of a job interview with the words in the box.

done • (x2) does • can • would • that (x2) • saying

Interviewer: Have you ever had to deal with difficult customers?
Candidate: Yes, I have ¹_____. I did ²_____ several times when I worked at Ainsworth's. Not that there were too many occasions!
Interviewer: And can you handle these situations?
Candidate: Yes, I ³_____. I always begin by listening to the customer. Listening is the key thing.
Interviewer: So you were ⁴_____ earlier. But how ⁵_____ it work here?
Candidate: Well, even if the customer was being very difficult, they would still have the right to express themselves.
Interviewer: Yes, they ⁶_____ do. But what happens after you've listened?
Candidate: Well, after I've ⁷_____ that, I basically work out as quickly as possible if the company can actually give the customer what they want.
Interviewer: Good. And if the company can't do ⁸_____?
Candidate: Then I would explain why not as politely as possible, referring to company policy, rules and so on.
Interviewer: Alright. Thank you, Mr Gregson. We'll be in touch shortly.

Extension

1 Look at Exercise 4 again and then write the dialogue the candidate had with his wife when he got home. She will ask lots of questions about the interview! Try to use some of the language you have studied in this unit.

2 Practise the dialogue in Exercise 4 and your new one, paying attention to stress and intonation.

7 SOUND MORE POLITE

About the language

> Excuse me, could you possibly move your car?   Sure. No problem.

Being polite means making your language less direct (often through past tenses) – and knowing how to respond to what other people say. It's such an important aspect of conversation that there is information about it throughout the book (see Units 3, 8, 16 and 18 in particular). But the purpose of this unit is to bring together in one place examples of the commonest verbs and phrases. Notice that in the examples below, the words in brackets make the sentences even less direct.

1 Could, would, mind

Before you read on, think about some of the ways you could make the request below more polite, using *could*, *would* and *mind* and any other 'softening' words/phrases. Check your answer on page 33.

> Please turn the volume down.

We use *could*, *would* and *mind* in requests and suggestions:

1. **Could you** (possibly) show me the way to Lecture Theatre 1 (please)?
2. **Would you** give me a call later (please)? I'm rather busy at the moment.
3. **Would/Do you mind** giving me a hand (please)?
4. **We could** have a look at the library now (if you like).
5. **Would you mind** having/if we had an early dinner tonight?

Note that when we're trying to persuade people, the negative form *Couldn't we* is even less direct than the positive form:

> **Could/Couldn't we** (perhaps) continue our discussion after lunch?

For offers, we use *would*:

> **Would** you like a coffee or some water?

If + *mind* at the start of a sentence will soften its impact:

1. **If you don't mind**, I won't come to the cinema tonight. I'm a bit tired.
2. **If you don't mind** me saying so, you're taking a risk with your money.

▶ Practice: Exercises 1, 2 and 3 pages 34–35.

2 Hope, think, wonder

We often use these three verbs in the past continuous to make requests:

1. **I was hoping** we could/might have a (quick) chat some time over the weekend.
2. **We were (just) wondering** if we could/might have some extra towels for our room.
3. **I was thinking** of having a bath (if that's okay)?

We can also use these verbs in other tenses:

1. **I hope** you don't mind if I borrow your shampoo?
2. **Do you think** you could let me have a (quick) look at your map?
3. **I wondered** if I could get you anything from the supermarket.

We sometimes use the future continuous, particularly to ask politely about people's short-term plans:

> **Will we be eating** before we go out?

▶ Practice: Exercise 4 page 35.

ABOUT THE LANGUAGE

3 *Please, possibly, excuse me, if you like, I'm afraid; thanks (very much), you're welcome; sorry, that's okay, oh dear*

Listen to the conversation below, which puts all of these words/phrases in context.

> **A:** **Excuse me**, I think you've dropped your gloves!
> **B:** **Oh dear**! I'm always doing that. **Thanks very much**.
> **A:** **You're welcome**. Would you like a hand with your bags?
> **B:** Yes, **please**. **I'm afraid** they're quite heavy. Do you live round here?
> **A:** Just up the road, yes.
> **B:** Could I **possibly** ask you something, then?
> **A:** Of course.
> **B:** Well, I'm going to stay in a friend's apartment near here and I was just wondering if it was, you know, a safe area to live in?
> **A:** Oh yes. It's a very quiet part of town. Are you from the States?
> **B:** Canada, actually.
> **A:** **Sorry**.
> **B:** **That's okay**. People always think I'm American.
> **A:** I can show you around a little, **if you like**. Tomorrow, perhaps?
> **B:** **Thanks**. That would be great.

Oh dear **is an expression we use instead of something more offensive. Can you think of other inoffensive expressions? And what could you say instead of** *You're welcome* **and** *That's okay***? Check your answers below.**

Apart from starting a sentence with *I'm afraid*, we also use *I'm afraid not* as a polite way of saying *No* and *I'm afraid so* for *Yes*:

> 1 **A:** Have you got the time, please?
>   **B:** (No,) **I'm afraid not**.
>
> 2 **A:** Excuse me, but have we just missed a bus?
>   **B:** **I'm afraid so.** There's another one in about twenty minutes, though.

Another way of saying *Could I ...* is *Perhaps I could ...*:

> **A:** I don't think I've got time for lunch.
> **B:** Oh dear. **Perhaps I could** make you a sandwich to take with you?

As well as using *sorry* to apologise, we use it (often with *but*) to soften requests:

> 1 **I'm sorry, but** could you possibly turn the volume down?
> 2 **Sorry** to be a nuisance/pain, **but** could you look something up for me on the internet?

▶ Practice: Exercise 5 page 35.

Answers

1 Could you possibly turn the volume down?/Would you turn the volume down a little bit, please?/Would you mind turning the volume down, please?

3 *Gosh!* and *Good grief!* are both as inoffensive as *Oh dear! No problem.* or *Any time.* or *It's a pleasure.* are other ways of saying *You're welcome.* You could say *That's alright.* or *Don't worry.* instead of *That's okay.*

33

7 SOUND MORE POLITE

Practice

1a Tick (✔) the sentences where you can use both *Could* and *Couldn't*. Put a cross (✘) if you can only use Could.

1. Could/Couldn't we perhaps keep the champagne for a special occasion?
2. Could/Couldn't you record the movie, and we'll watch it later?
3. Could/Couldn't you tell me the time, please?
4. Could/Couldn't I finish what I'm doing and meet you later?
5. Could/Couldn't you give me a discount on that fridge? It seems expensive.
6. Could/Couldn't you possibly tell me where the nearest cash machine is?

b Listen and <u>underline</u> the alternative you hear.

c Add a suitable answer a–f to the questions/statements 1–6 above.

a Of course. Come to *Milly's Café*. I'll be there.
b Sure. It's outside the supermarket at the end of this street.
c Of course. It's my birthday next week, so maybe we can open it then?
d Okay. What about 10% off?
e Sure. It's half-past ten.
f I don't know. Why can't you just sit down, and we'll watch it together now?

2 The phrases in bold in these e-mails are in the wrong places. Put them in the correct places.

Subject: BBQ

Hi Kes
if you don't mind if you and your family fancied coming over on Sunday afternoon. **Hope** of having a barbecue. **would you mind** you'll be able to make it? Rick

---

Subject: re. BBQ

Hey Rick
Thanks for your e-mail. We'd love to come over, but there's a slight problem – Jo's mum's staying with us for the weekend, **We were thinking** her coming, that'd be great. Also, she won't be able to leave her dog at home, so **I was wondering** if the dog comes too? **Do you think** you don't think I'm being rude – let me know. Kes

---

3a Put the words in the dialogues in the correct order. Use punctuation as appropriate.

> The modals in Exercise 3 are usually pronounced in their weak forms (schwa, /ə/) and are always unstressed.

1 **A:** like some tea / would you?
   Would you like some tea?
   B: yes please / oh
   Oh, yes please.

2 **A:** my e-mails / if I checked / would you mind ?

   B: no / problem / sure

3 **A:** for me / opening a window / would you mind

   B: not at all / no

4 **A:** call me / a taxi / would you?

   B: I'll do it now / yes

5 **A:** if you don't mind / leave the conference early / I'd like to

   B: be alright / that should

6 **A:** in here please / not smoking / do you mind

   B: I'll put it out / oh sorry

b Listen to check your answers. Then listen again and repeat.

PRACTICE

4a Complete these sentences with the words/phrases in the box.

was hoping • hope • were wondering • was thinking • think • mind • don't mind • would you

1 We _____ if we could borrow the car tonight.
2 I _____ of asking John to look at the washing machine – he's really good at fixing things.
3 I've finished off the milk. I _____ you don't mind.
4 Would you _____ feeding my cat while I'm away?
5 Do you _____ you could open the window? It's so hot.
6 I _____ to catch the 5 o'clock train, but I'm so busy, I don't think I'll be home until late.
7 If you _____ me saying so, I thought you were rude to that customer.
8 The doctor's free at 2.30. _____ be able to come then?

b Match the sentences 1–8 above to the likely speakers a–h.

a doctor's receptionist __8__
b neighbour _____
c colleagues in a shop _____
d friends _____
e flatmates _____
f teenager to parent _____
g commuters on a bus _____
h married couple _____

5 There are eight words missing in the dialogue below. Insert the words in the box in the correct places and make any necessary changes to capital letters.

me • thank • ~~oh~~ • I'm • you're • sorry • so • could

    Oh d
A: ~~D~~ear, what have I done with my glasses? Where are they?!
B: Excuse are these yours? I found them on the floor near the toilets.
A: Oh, you!
B Welcome.
A: Afraid I'm not very awake today. I've just lost my purse. I'm sure it's somewhere here in the library, but I can't find it anywhere.
B: I've got a bit of time to spare, so I could help you look, if you like.
A: That would be so kind of you. You possibly look round those bookshelves over there for me while I check here again? To be a nuisance!
B: I know how it feels to have a bad day. I'll meet you back here in a few minutes.
A: That's great. Thanks much.

Extension

1 Write short dialogues for the situations 1–3.

1 You want to go on holiday with your friends but need some money. Who do you talk to about this problem and what do you say to them?
2 You see an old lady in the street having problems crossing the road. You offer to help, and you get into a conversation with her. What do you say to each other?
3 You've been invited to a friend's wedding, but you really don't want to go. What do you say to your friend?

2 Record yourself telling this story. Think about pauses and intonation.

35

8 BE VAGUE WITH *THING/THINGY*, AND *THINGS (LIKE THAT)*, ETC.

About the language

> Shall we watch that thing on TV?   No, I've got some tidying and stuff to do.

Vague means 'not precise/exact'. Spoken language is often vague. We don't always have time to be precise – and being vague can be a more relaxed way of speaking to people. In this unit and in Unit 9, we look at some of the key vague language.

1 *Thing, thingy* and *things*

In the two sentences below, think of some examples of what the 'things' and 'thing' mentioned could actually be. Then check your answers on page 37.

1 I can't find my sports **things** anywhere.
2 I've got a **thing** on at work tonight, so I might be late.

Thing is a very common vague word. We often say it because we don't want to use, or we can't think of, a more exact word:

A: Look. I've got this **thing** on my leg.
B: You poor **thing**, Sam. Does it hurt?

The thing on the boy's leg might be an insect bite. But sometimes the meaning of *thing* is not so clear:

A: There was a **thing** at the office today.
B: Really? What sort of **thing**?

The use of *thing* here suggests something unusual – but it could be anything from an 'argument' or 'some news' to 'a party'.

Sometimes we use *thingy/thingies* (or *thingamajig* or *thingummy*) instead of *thing*:

1 Where's the **thingy** for cleaning the window?
2 Did you send a Christmas card to **thingy**?

We normally use *thingy* rather than *thing* for people, except in the expression *You poor/stupid/brave/clever **thing***.

Thingy can sometimes replace an adjective:

> It's a **thingy** infection – you know, one you can catch just by coming into contact with people. (the speaker means 'contagious'.)

The word *things* can be quite vague:

1 Shall we call a meeting, or shall we just see how **things** develop? (*things* = 'the situation')
2 **Things** aren't good between us. (We're having problems in our relationship.)

Things can simply mean 'our personal belongings':

1 Have you packed your holiday **things** yet?
2 You can put your **things** in the spare room, if you like.

Both *thing* and *things* are used in many common expressions such as:

1 How are **things**?
2 I haven't got a **thing** to wear.
3 **Things** can only get better.
4 I don't know the first **thing** about cars. (I don't know anything about cars.)

▶ Practice: Exercises 1, 2 and 3 pages 38–39.

ABOUT THE LANGUAGE

2 And things/stuff (like that), and everything, or something

In the following dialogue, try to replace the <u>underlined</u> part with one word. Check your answer below.

> **A:** Where's Nina?
> **B:** She's gone for a walk or <u>to see a friend or to buy some milk</u>.

The phrase *and things (like that)* means 'and other things which are similar':

> In the evenings I like to play music, watch TV **and things like that**.

You can use the more informal word *stuff* instead of *things*, and you don't have to say *like that* at the end:

> **A:** Did you get much shopping done?
> **B:** Well, I got a few CDs **and stuff**, but nothing useful.

The phrase *and everything* is more emphatic than *and things/stuff (like that)*. It means 'and the other things that complete the idea, or make a complete idea stronger':

> He's rich. His family's got a yacht **and everything**.

You could use *and things* in the example above, but it doesn't work with an idea that already seems complete:

> They're a couple now. They're in love and ~~things~~ everything.

The phrase *or something* means 'or something similar'. It is different from *and things/stuff*, because we are talking about **one** alternative action rather than a list of things:

> **A:** Where's Pete?
> **B:** I don't know. He's walking the dog ~~and things~~ **or something**.

In negative sentences we normally use *or anything* instead of *or something*:

> It was my birthday and he didn't send me a card **or anything**.

We can use all these expressions after nouns:

1 If we want a picnic, we'll need **bread and fruit** and things.
2 **A:** Who's Mo Baker?
  B: She's a **pop star** or something.

We can also use them after verbs/verb phrases:

1 Why is everyone running? Is there a train **coming** or something?
2 On our holidays we sailed and **swam** and everything! It was great!

Listen to the dialogues and notice the intonation. Then listen and repeat.

1 **A:** Are you hungry? Do you fancy a sandwich or something?
  B: I'd like one of those thingies you made last week.
  A: A panini? Sure. What sort of filling? I've got tuna and ham and stuff like that.

2 **A:** What are you doing in the holidays?
  B: Ian's invited me to go sailing in the Mediterranean on his yacht. I'll be able to see Sicily and the Greek islands and everything! What about you?
  A: Nothing much, I'm afraid. I've got to finish a couple of essays and things.

▶ Practice: Exercises 4 and 5 page 39.

Answers

1 *things*: e.g.: trainers, football boots, track suit, swimming trunks, etc.
  thing: special event such as a product launch or a leaving party, etc.
2 something

8 BE VAGUE WITH *THING/THINGY*, AND *THINGS (LIKE THAT)*, ETC.

Practice

1 Underline the correct alternative to complete the sentences.

1 I haven't seen you for ages! How are *thingy/thing/things*?
2 *Thing/Things/Thingy* haven't been very good at work lately.
3 There was this *thing/thingy/things* on Oxford Street today. The road was blocked for ages!
4 We need some of those *thing/thingy/thingies* for hanging pictures up with.
5 Have you seen *thingy/thing/things* lately? You know, Mimi's boyfriend.
6 You don't need to go home for your sports *things/thingy/thing*. I can lend you some.

2 Use the words in the box to complete the dialogue.

thing (x2) • thingy (x2) • things (x2)

Ann: So Pete was telling me that he met up with ¹ *thingy* last week – you know, the girl with the long red hair. Anyway, talk about a nightmare holiday, she went up to Liverpool to see her family, but before she even got there someone stole her ² _____ on the train while she was in the toilet.
Tim: Oh no, poor ³ _____!
Ann: Well, ⁴ _____ got even worse when she arrived, 'cause she found that her mum had caught this awful ⁵ _____ from someone she worked with, and so the whole family was ill! They were all sent to hospital, and had to stay in one of those ⁶ _____ wards, where you're kept apart from everyone else.
Ann: Gosh! How awful.

3 Choose the best the vague word in brackets to replace a two-word phrase in the dialogues 1–4.

1 A: Jim, can you call Jess back? There's a ~~small matter~~ *thing* she'd like to discuss.
   B: Okay, will do. Do you know what it is? (<u>thing</u>/thingy)

2 A: I got this funny machine for Christmas. It wakes you up and makes a cup of tea!
   B: Amazing! Wish I had one! (thingummy/things)

3 A: Did you get a party invitation in the post from Jenny?
   B: Yeah, I got one this morning. (thing/thingy)

4 A: There was a special event in the town square today.
   B: Oh! What was that? (thingummy/thing)

4a Match 1–5 with a–e to make sentences.

1 I got some chocolates, clothes   a snacky things like that?
2 Watched a DVD, had something to eat and   b stuff like that.
3 Oh, he likes cinema, galleries and   c and nice stuff like that.
4 How about some crisps, nuts and   d arty things like that.
5 Don't worry! Only that you're funny, sweet – e did some stuff round the house.

b Match the questions a–e to the 'answers' 1–5 above.

a What did he say about me?
b What's he into?
c What shall I bring to the party?
d What did you get for your birthday?
e What did you get up to last night?

> *To be into* means 'be interested in'.

PRACTICE

5a <u>Underline</u> the correct alternative to complete the sentences.

1 Jack married into money and he's got a big house, a villa in Spain <u>and everything</u>/or something !
2 Pete's dad's in finance and everything/or something. I can never remember.
3 I think my boss is on leave and everything/or something.
4 They're definitely a couple! They got married and everything/and things like that!
5 The car's broken down. It won't start or anything/or something .
6 I got a new computer last week. It's got a modem, memory stick, speakers and everything/or something.

(22) **b** Listen to check your answers. Notice the intonation pattern. Does it go up or down at the end of each sentence? Listen again and repeat.

6a Look at the pictures A–F and make a note of what you think the person is saying, using vague language.

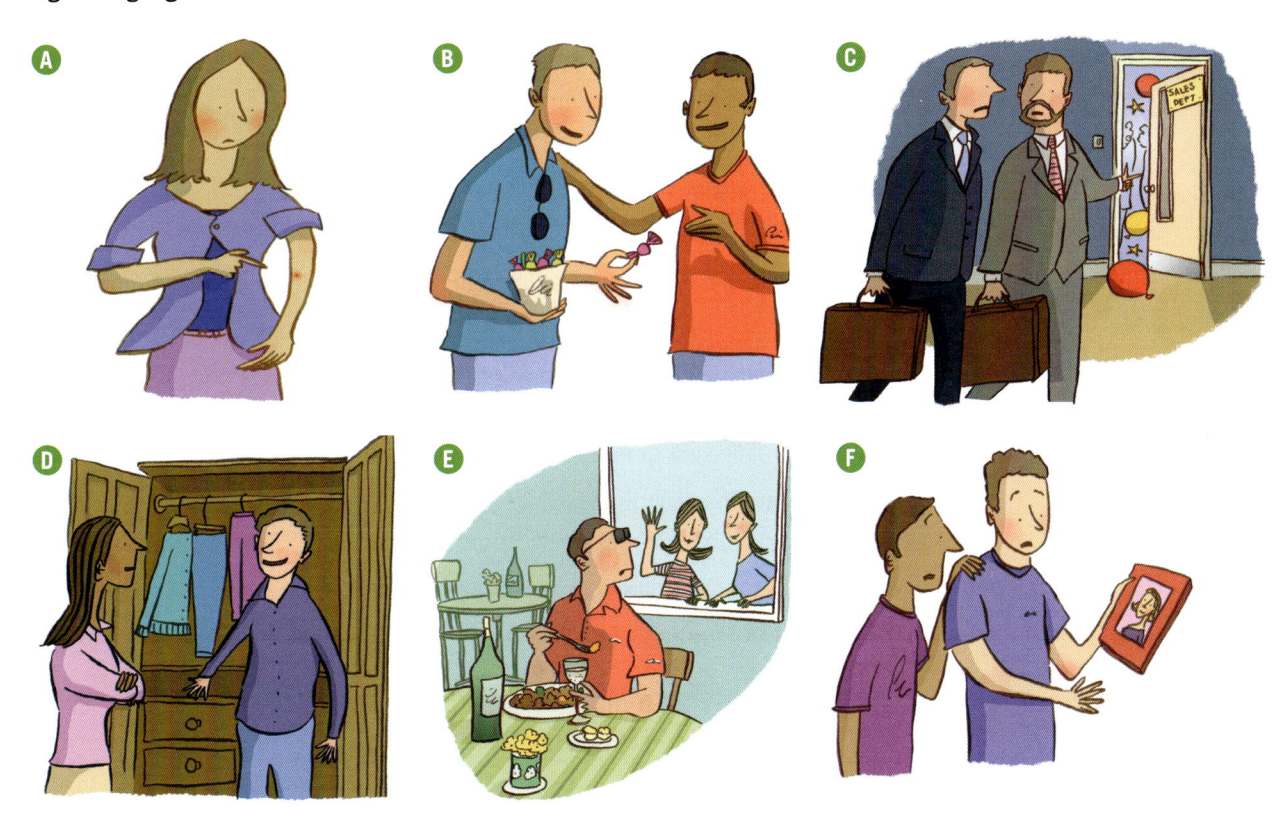

b Match the pictures A–F to the sentences 1–5.

1 Look in there! Isn't that thingy who was in that film?
2 Have a thingy!
3 Do you want to put your things in there?
4 There's a thing going on in there.
5 We used to have a thing.
6 Look, I've got this thing on my arm!

Extension

Think about the questions below. Imagine you are going to talk about them to someone else. Try to use some vague words/phrases.

1 Think of a time when you didn't have a thing to wear. What did you do?
2 Has there been a time when things haven't gone well for you at work/school/college? What happened?
3 Have you ever had your things stolen while you were travelling? Did you get them back?
4 Are any of your friends having a thing?
5 What things do you usually take to parties?

9 BE VAGUE AGAIN WITH *SORT OF, KIND OF, A COUPLE OF,* ETC.

About the language

> Your uncle is a **sort of** doctor, isn't he?
>
> As mentioned in Unit 8, *vague* means 'not precise/exact'. Spoken language is often vague. We don't always have time to be precise – and being vague can be a more relaxed way of speaking to people. In this unit, we look at some more vague language.

1 *Sort of, kind of*

There are two meanings for the phrase *sort of/kind of*. The first is 'type of':

> 1 A: What **sort/kind/type of** dog does she have?
>   B: I'm pretty sure it's an Alsatian.
>
> 2 A: What **sort of** conversation did you have with him?
>   B: Well, he was a bit angry, but it was okay.

The second and 'vague' meaning is 'not exactly'. We often use these words to make our language less direct, and to give us time to think.

Listen and notice and the pronunciation in the dialogues. Then listen and repeat.

> 1 A: What happened to you yesterday?
>   B: I was feeling **kind of** ill, so I went home.
>
> 2 A: Are you looking forward to the weekend?
>   B: **Sort of**. I've got quite a lot of work to do, but I should get a break on Sunday.
>
> 3 A: How are things at work?
>   B: Well, it's been **sort of**, you know, **kind of** tense since Tim left.

Sort of/kind of can be followed by a verb form, as well as an adjective or a noun:

> I was **sort of hoping** you might come to the hospital with me this afternoon.

Note that *kind of* tends to be more popular with American English speakers.

▶ Practice: Exercise 1 page 42.

2 *(A) bit (of), a couple of, loads of*

What words could you use to replace *bit*, *bits*, *a bit of a* in the sentences below? Check your answers on page 41.

> 1 I'm a **bit** tired today.
> 2 Be careful. There are some **bits** of glass on the floor.
> 3 You'll enjoy the Pembrokeshire coast, but it's **a bit of a** journey.

The word *bit* has a relaxed, informal feel to it. As an adverb, it means 'a little':

> 1 That's **a bit** expensive, isn't it?
> 2 Shall we wait **a bit**?

As a noun, it means 'a small piece':

> 1 I enjoyed some **bits** of the film.
> 2 You haven't painted the **bit** by the sink.

Sometimes the meaning can be negative:

> I thought he was **a bit** rude.

ABOUT THE LANGUAGE

We often use the phrase *a bit of* before uncountable (concrete and abstract) nouns:

1   There's **a bit of** cheese left in the fridge.
2   Can we have **a bit of** peace around here, please?

Before singular countable nouns, *a bit of a* is often an understatement meaning 'quite a lot'.

There's **a bit of a** queue, I'm afraid. (There's quite a long queue.)

A couple of normally means 'a few', and is a fairly common 'vague' expression in conversation:

I bumped into Mark on Oxford Street **a couple of** weeks ago.

Load(s) is a common alternative to *lot(s)* in spoken English, and has a slightly more emphatic meaning. The most common use is in the phrase *loads of* (with countable and uncountable nouns):

1   You won't get bored. There's **loads of** things to do in the evening.
2   I'd like to come, but I've got **loads of** work to do this weekend.

The singular form *a load of* is often used in negative expressions:

1   She said she didn't have time, but I think that's **a load of** rubbish.
2   What **a load of** nonsense!

▶ **Practice: Exercises 2, 3 and 5 pages 42–43.**

3   *-ish* and *-y*

What's the meaning of the phrases in bold? Check your answers below.

That's Mike over there. The **shortish** guy in the **greeny-brown** jacket.

The suffixes *-ish* and *-y* make some nouns into regular adjectives:

fool**ish**, child**ish**, Swed**ish**, book**ish** ('fond of reading and study')
sand**y**, wealth**y**, shak**y**, sport**y** ('fond of/good at sport')

We also use these suffixes, as part of our vague, less formal language to mean 'approximately'. The suffix *-ish* is more common, and is generally used with measurements, numbers and times, while *-y* can be used with materials:

1   I'm not sure how old he is. **Fortyish** perhaps?
2   The food is wonderful, but the restaurant itself is a bit **plasticky**.

Both, however, are used with colours:

1   It's not exactly blue. It's more of a **bluey-pink** I would say.
2   The water was rather **brownish**, so we didn't drink it.

They are also used in more creative ways, generally with adjectives:

1   It wasn't a bad film, but it was bit **slowish** for a comedy.
2   She's got a painting in her room which is a bit **Chinesey**.

The choice of *-ish* or *-y* in these cases often depends on the ending of the word, and which sounds more comfortable. You would say *strawberryish taste* not *strawberry-y*, for example, and *Spanishy sort of food* rather than *Spanishish*!

▶ **Practice: Exercise 4 page 41.**

Answers

2   *bit* = little; *bits* = small pieces; *a bit of a* = quite a long (journey).
3   *shortish* = quite short; *greeny-brown* = a mixture of green and brown.

9 BE VAGUE AGAIN WITH *SORT OF, KIND OF, A COUPLE OF,* ETC.

Practice

1a Mark the sentences T if *kind of/sort of* means 'type of' and V if it means 'vaguely'.

1 What sort of car are you going to buy?
2 Well, they're kind of going out together.
3 What kind of doctor is he?
4 What kind of time is best for you? Evening?
5 Oh, he's a sort of nurse; he works at a local practice.
6 I want something kind of small and practical, that I can park easily.
7 Sort of any time really. I haven't made plans.
8 What kind of holiday are you having this year?
9 I'm kind of thinking about camping this year, to save a bit of money.
10 What sort of friend is she exactly?

b Put sentences 1–10 into five pairs, with a question and an answer in each pair.

1 _1, 6_   2 _____   3 _____   4 _____   5 _____

2 Match 1–10 with a–j to complete what the speaker is saying.

1 I'm in a bit of a hurry.   a It looks delicious.
2 I'm feeling a bit tired this afternoon.   b but it's not really my thing.
3 Shall we just wait here for a bit –   c when I saw Sally and Tim together.
4 I've got a bit of free time this morning.   d I'm running late for work.
5 Some bits of this book are okay –   e I think it's something I ate.
6 Shall we have a bit of that cake?   f I hope she breaks up with him!
7 I've got a bit of a stomach ache.   g a taxi is bound to come in a minute.
8 I got a bit upset   h He loves the sound of his own voice!
9 He's a bit of an idiot.   i I need a coffee to wake me up.
10 He does go on a bit.   j Fancy getting together?

> *Go on a bit* means 'talk too much'.

3 <u>Underline</u> the correct alternative to complete the sentences.

1 I'm only staying *a couple/loads* of weeks so I won't be able to see much of the country.
2 He owes me *a couple/loads* of money now, so I hope he can pay me back.
3 I need to make *a couple/loads of* phone calls. I won't be long.
4 *A couple/Loads* of people applied for the job, so it was very difficult to choose.
5 Barcelona's so great for culture. There are *a couple/loads* of galleries, museums and churches!
6 It's not a very green city. There are *a couple/loads* of parks, but that's all.
7 She's got *a couple/loads* of cats – how does she keep them all in her tiny one-bedroom flat?
8 He only gave me *loads/a couple* of pounds, so I couldn't buy more than one ice cream.

PRACTICE

4a Replace the phrases in bold with a word ending in *-ish* or *-y*.

1. I'm not sure but I think he's **around the age of thirty**.   _Thirtyish_
2. He's very quiet and **the sort of person who reads a lot**. _____
3. This **nylon-type** material is too hot for this weather. _____
4. The party starts at eight but I think we should get there at **around 9 o'clock**. _____
5. **A:** What does he look like?
   B: Well, **he's fairly short**, with grey hair. _____
6. He's very **keen on sport** – he plays a lot of football and tennis. _____
7. **A:** What's the food like?
   B: It's **similar to Italian**, with lots of pasta and sauces. _____
8. **A:** What's the club like?
   B: Well, most people are **quite young** and fashionable. _____
9. It's got a very strong **mint-type** taste. _____
10. **A:** What colour's his hair?
    B: Well, it's got **a bit of grey**. _____

b Listen and check your answers. Notice the pronunciation of the words ending in *-ish* and *-y*.

5 Complete the sentence stems 1–3 with words/phrases from the box.

shopping • upset • small jobs around the house (x2) • under the weather
paperwork • things at the office (x2) • work this weekend • tired

1. I've got to do loads of _shopping._
   _____.
   _____.
   _____.

2. I'm feeling a bit _____.
   _____.
   _____.

3. I've got to do a couple of _____.
   _____.

Extension

1. Write a dialogue using sentences from Exercise 5 above.

2. Think about the answers to these questions.

   1. What sort of films are you into?
   2. What would be your dream kind of holiday?
   3. What sort of things do you do to relax?
   4. What kind of people do you admire?
   5. When was the last time you felt a bit of an idiot? Why? What happened?
   6. When did you last get a bit upset? What about?
   7. Have you ever lent somebody loads of money? Did you get it back?
   8. Do you know anyone who's sporty? Bookish? Babyish?

10 SAY LESS

About the language

> *Expensive*, aren't they? Are you going to buy one?   Well, I'd like to.

Ellipsis means leaving out (not saying) words when your meaning is clear without them. It is a natural part of conversation, not only because it saves time, but also because it 'links' what we say to what our partner has said. In Unit 1 (page 4), we saw some examples in questions: ~~Are there~~ Any messages for me? Another frequent example is in 'short answers': *A: Are you leaving right now? B: Yes, I am. ~~leaving right now~~*. In this unit, we'll look at other common types of ellipsis.

1 Ellipsis at the beginning of sentences

Read this short conversation, and try to write down the missing words at the beginning of each line. Then check your answers on page 45.

> A: Going anywhere in the summer?
> B: Don't know yet. We might visit my wife's parents in Portugal. What about you?
> A: Depends. If my company sends me to America in June, I might stay on for a couple of weeks.
> B: Wish my company would send me abroad sometimes.

Below are some common words you can sometimes leave out at the start of sentences. Note, however, that if you do this too often, or in more formal situations, it might sound rude.

I *('m/'ve/'d)*, We *('re/'ve/'d)*

1 A: ~~I~~ Love your red laptop!
  B: It's great, isn't it?

2 A: Are you feeling okay?
  B: ~~I've~~ Got a headache again, I'm afraid.

3 A: Where are you?
  B: ~~I'm~~ On the train.

4 A: Would you like a coffee?
  B: ~~I'd~~ Better not. I've had three already.

5 A: ~~We~~ Need some more milk, if you're going to the shops.
  B: Okay, I'll get some.

Are *(you)*, Do *(you)*, Have *(you)*

1 ~~Are you~~ Ready yet?
2 ~~Do~~ You want an ice cream?
3 ~~Have you~~ Finished?

It *('s a)*, That *(+ be)*

1 A: ~~It's~~ Hot today, isn't it?
  B: Yes. ~~It's a~~ Pity we didn't bring a picnic.

2 A: Can you meet me when you're in Paris?
  B: ~~It~~ Depends. It Might be difficult.

3 You're going to New York in March? ~~That~~ Sounds exciting.

4 A: You must be tired after that journey.
  B: ~~That's~~ True. I'm exhausted.

ABOUT THE LANGUAGE

This type of ellipsis is sometimes followed by a question tag:

Been waiting long, **have you**?

Terrible match, **wasn't it**?

> We often leave out the first words in expressions we use at the end of conversations: I'll See you later! I'll Talk to you tomorrow. I've Got to go now.

▶ Practice: Exercises 1, 2 and 5 pages 46–47.

2 Ellipsis later in sentences

As with 'short answers', we don't need to repeat information after modal verbs:

1 If anyone can help him, George can. ~~help him.~~

2 **A:** I wouldn't buy anything at that market.
  B: Oh, I would. ~~buy something.~~ It's fun.

3 **A:** I might go the gym this evening.
  B: If you think it will help you relax, you should. ~~go to the gym.~~

With the verbs *ask, hope, would like, would love, need,* and *want* we don't need to repeat the infinitive clauses after *to*.

Listen and notice the word stress at the end of the responses by speaker B.

1 **A:** Is Fred going to give us a lift tonight?
  B: Well, I asked him to. ~~give us a lift.~~

2 **A:** Would you like to come skiing with us next month?
  B: Of course. I'd love to. ~~come skiing.~~

3 **A:** You don't have to buy me a present this year.
  B: I know, but I want to. ~~buy you a present.~~

▶ Practice this form of ellipsis in Exercise 3 on page 46.

3 Ellipsis with prepositions

What are the prepositions that have been left out in the two examples below? Check your answers below.

1 She's been away two days now. Do you think she's okay?
2 Why don't you come round Sunday morning?

We sometimes leave out the prepositions *at, for, in, on, to*:

1 **A:** When does your plane leave?
  B: ~~At~~ Six o'clock.

2 **A:** Where is Dundee?
  B: ~~In~~ Scotland.

3 **A:** You're in a hurry. Where are you going?
  B: ~~To~~ The station. See you later!

▶ Practice: 4 page 47.

Answers

1 Are you (Going anywhere…); I (Don't know yet.); It (Depends.); I (Wish my…).
3 She's been away ~~for~~ two days now. Why don't you come round ~~on~~ Sunday morning?

45

10 SAY LESS

Practice

1 Cross out the words you don't need at the beginning of the sentences.

1 **A:** Where are you?
   B: ~~I'm~~ on the bus, Jo.
2 Are there any of those chocolate biscuits left? The ones in the tin.
3 It's freezing today, isn't it?
4 **A:** What's the matter? You look awful!
   B: I've got a cold, again.
5 **A:** Are you coming to the party tonight?
   B: Yes, I can't wait.
6 **A:** Have you got a light please?
   B: Sorry, no, I don't smoke.
7 **A:** So I asked her to marry me!
   B: That's great! What did she say?
8 Have you ever been to San José?

2a Complete the statements 1–5 with the correct question tags a–e.

1 Awful weather today,   a aren't we?
2 Terrible play yesterday,   b isn't she?
3 Happy now,   c isn't it?
4 Free on Saturday night,   d wasn't it?
5 Really great teacher,   e are you?

b Use your answers above to complete the dialogues 1–5.

1 **A:** _____
   B: Yeah, I'm learning so much this term.
2 **A:** _____
   B: Why? What's the plan?
3 **A:** _____
   B: Yes, now I've got what I want!
4 **A:** _____
   B: I know, but it's supposed to get nicer later.
5 **A:** _____
   B: Oh yeah, the acting was awful.

3 Write the information that has been left out after the responses in bold.

1 **A:** Have you booked your holiday yet?
   B: No, **I haven't**. I've been too busy.   _booked my holiday_
2 **A:** That shop is so over-priced!
   B: No **it isn't**. There are lots of bargains.   _____
3 **A:** I've never been to Spain before.
   B: Really? **You should go**. It's great.   _____
4 **A:** Would you like to come with me to the opera?
   B: Oh, **I'd love to**.   _____
5 **A:** Do you think I should buy Jim a birthday present?
   B: **I wouldn't**, you've only known him for two days. _____
6 **A:** You don't have to pay for me, you know.
   B: I know, but **I want to**.   _____

PRACTICE

4 Cross out the prepositions that you don't need in the dialogues.

1 **A:** What time does your class start?
 B: ~~At~~ two.

2 **A:** How long is your girlfriend away?
 B: For three days. Fancy coming over one evening?

3 **A:** Let's go out on Saturday night.
 B: Can't, I'm afraid. I'm working.

4 **A:** Where has she gone on holiday?
 B: To Spain. Not quite sure whereabouts though.

5 **A:** Where's he staying at the moment?
 B: At our place.

6 **A:** How long have you known Annabel?
 B: For ages!

5a Dora and Luis are working out what they need at the supermarket. Write in numbers where they've left out words, and put the words at the end, as in the example.

Dora: So, what do we need then?
Luis: 1 Everything really. Think we should stock up because we can borrow my mum's car.
Dora: Good point. Okay, so all the usual things – bread, cheese. Eggs?
Luis: Yeah. Run out of eggs, so we'll need a dozen.
Dora: Okay. What about coffee?
Luis: Yeah. Running quite low. Need a couple of packets.
Dora: Milk?
Luis: Completely out, so put that down – two litres, yeah?
Dora: Sounds good. What about fruit and veg?
Luis: Need lots. Got your brother coming, haven't we?
Dora: Yeah. What about tins?
Luis: Get a few more. Beans, tuna – always useful.
Dora: Got much pasta?
Luis: Let's see. Oh yeah. Got a bit, only enough for one though, so let's get more.
Dora: Right, let's see what we've got so far: bread, cheese, a dozen eggs …

1   *We need*

> *Stock up* means 'get a full supply of something essential'.
> *Put that down* means 'write those words on paper'.

b Listen to the questions Dora asks Luis and decide whether her intonation goes up or down at the end. Are there any patterns?

Extension

Read out your version of Exercise 4 with all the added words. Compare it with the recorded version. Which do you think sounds better? Why?

11 EXAGGERATE!

About the language

> These shoes are killing me!   Don't worry. We'll be home soon.

Exaggerated language (sometimes called *hyperbole*) is very common in informal conversation, particularly amongst teenagers, and when we're gossiping or telling stories. Apart from frequently-used verbs like *kill* and *die* (for example, *I'm dying for a cold drink*), and expressions such as *I'm so hungry I could eat a horse/my plate/the table* exaggerations tend to occur when we talk about numbers or amounts, and time and space. We'll look at these two areas in this unit, and also at the role of extreme adjectives and adverbs, and understatement.

1 Numbers/Amounts

In the two examples below, the person speaking is clearly exaggerating. What would you guess are the realistic numbers? Check your answers on page 49.

1. I've got **a million** e-mails in my inbox.
2. There are **thousands** of books to read for this exam.

The number expressions that we use most frequently in exaggerated language are *dozens of*, *hundreds of/a hundred*, *thousands of* and *millions of/a million*.

(27) Listen and notice how the stress falls on the number in the examples below.

1. Sorry I'm late. There were dozens of people waiting for the lift.
2. You've got hundreds of phone messages, by the way.
3. I can think of a hundred reasons why you shouldn't see him anymore.
4. There are thousands of mistakes in this essay.
5. I wanted to get us tickets, but there were millions of people in the queue.
6. I'd love to come but I've got a million things to get done.

The phrase *loads of* is so common that it isn't really seen as an exaggeration. *Tons of*, *masses of* and *piles of* are a little stronger:

1. There are **tons of** books in the flat that you never look at.
2. There was **masses of** food left over at the party.
3. We've got **piles of** washing-up to do. Can you give me a hand?

▶ Practice: Exercise 1 page 50.

2 Time and space

How do you think you could 'exaggerate' the underlined parts of these two statements? Check your answers on page 49.

1. Could you stand closer, please? You're a long way apart at the moment.
2. Can I talk to you for a very short time?

Years and *hours* are the commonest 'time' words – but *months*, *weeks*, *days*, *minutes* and *seconds* are also used in exaggerations. For some reason, we tend to use the numbers 'two' and 'five' with minutes and seconds:

1. It's tasty, but it needs **years** in the oven.
2. But it'll only take you **two minutes** to paint the bathroom!
3. Just give me **five seconds** of your time.

Despite the introduction of the metric system (kilometres, hectares, etc.), we still tend to use *miles* and *acres* (an acre is about 4050 square metres) in 'space' exaggerations:

1. You'd better walk a bit quicker. We've still got **miles** to go.
2. Of course we can have a party here. We've got **acres** of space in the living-room.

▶ Practice: Exercise 2 page 50.

ABOUT THE LANGUAGE

3 Extreme adjectives and adverbs

The adjective *endless* and the adverb *everywhere* are common in exaggerations:

1 That lecture was **endless**, wasn't it? I almost gave up the will to live.
2 Those new phone ads are **everywhere**, aren't they?

Adjectives of size such as *huge, massive, enormous, vast, gigantic* are also common:

There's a **gigantic** spider in the bath.

Such language is so common that it is not always recognised as exaggeration, and may be intensified by the adverb *absolutely*:

The pizzas they serve at Luigi's are **absolutely** vast.

The adjectives *absolute* and *total* are used in a similar, intensifying way:

1 I've got an **absolute** mountain of paperwork to do.
2 My boss is a **total** slave-driver!

Notice the following collocations: *an absolute fortune, absolute agony, a total disaster/ failure*.

The adverb *literally* is also used to make an exaggeration stronger:

I'm so tired I could **literally** sleep for years.

▶ Practice: Exercise 3 page 51.

4 Understatement

Understatement serves the same purpose of emphasis.

Listen and notice the intonation in these examples.

1 **A:** I think we've got a tiny, little problem here.
  B: What do you mean?
  A: Well, it looks like someone has stolen the car.

2 **A:** A female chief executive can never have the same authority as a man.
  B: Really? Well, I think we may have slightly different views on that.

3 **A:** How was your meal?
  B: Well, it wasn't the most interesting menu in the world.

A common form of understatement follows the pattern below:

He's **not the** bright**est** student in the class, I'm afraid.

▶ Practice: Exercise 4 page 51.

Answers

1 fifty e-mails; ten or fifteen books
2 miles apart; a second/minute

11 EXAGERATE!

Practice

1a Solve the anagram in brackets to complete the sentences.

1 I must have told you a _million_ times to pay the phone bill. (oillimn)
2 There were _____ of them and they all seemed really talented. (zedosn)
3 It's a bit of a nightmare actually, I've got to read _____ of books every week. (hustoands)
4 Yeah, but she doesn't need to wear _____ of make-up, she's already very beautiful. (lipse)
5 I'm just so fed-up with my housemates. They leave _____ of mess everywhere. (nots)
6 Yes, there were _____ of people protesting outside the Town Hall. (assmes)
7 Sorry, I can't, I've got a _____ things to do this evening. (illmoin)
8 We've got _____ of food in the kitchen! (sasmes)

1a Add a suitable lead-in a–h to the responses 1–8 above.

a Did many turn up for the auditions today?
b What's up?
c Are you still coming tonight?
d How's the course going?
e Don't you think she looks lovely?
f They've disconnected us!
g Is there anything to eat? I'm starving.
h Did you hear about the demonstration today?

2 Underline the most likely alternative to complete the dialogues.

1 **A:** Can you have a quick word with a customer about a discount? It'll only take two *seconds/days*.
   B: Sure. Put her through, will you?
2 **A:** Stop moaning, it'll only take you two *minutes/months* to mow the lawn!
   B: But my back's hurting!
3 **A:** It's already 9p.m. and we've got *miles/weeks* to walk before we get to the hotel.
   B: Okay, shall we try and get a cab?
4 **A:** We've been together for ten years now!
   B: I know, but it only feels like *weeks/years*, doesn't it?
5 **A:** Didn't you get my birthday card?
   B: No, but the post is really slow here, things take *years/hours* to arrive.
6 **A:** That lecture was so boring. It seemed to go on for *seconds/hours*!
   B: I know. I fell asleep at one point.
7 **A:** Can I have a quick word?
   B: Just give me five *seconds/hours* and I'll be with you.
8 Can you hurry up? You've been in that bathroom for *weeks/minutes* now!

PRACTICE

3a Complete the dialogues with an adjective or adverb from the box.

endless • absolute • fortune • literally • complete • everywhere • absolutely • massive • agony

1. **A:** My job's really getting me down. It's just _____ paperwork.
   B: It does sound _____ awful. I think you should look for something else.
2. **A:** How was the trip?
   B: It was an _____ disaster. I lost my passport and couldn't get any money out.
3. **A:** That Stewart Lee, he's _____ at the moment.
   B: Yes, he is, that's because he's got a new TV series. It's being advertised all over the place.
4. **A:** Are you going to get a new car then?
   B: No way! The holiday cost me an absolute _____ so we can't afford one.
5. **A:** Have you met her new boyfriend?
   B: Yes, he's a _____ idiot. I don't know what she sees in him.
6. **A:** I heard you've hurt your back. Are you okay?
   B: No, it's absolute _____.
7. **A:** They've got a _____ new flat screen TV.
   B: Yes, I saw it, it's vast, it takes up the whole living room.
8. **A:** He's so lazy.
   B: I know, I mean he _____ hasn't moved from that chair all day.

> If something *gets you down*, it makes you feel unhappy or depressed. We often use it to describe our work, other people's behaviour or the weather!

b Listen to the following extreme adjective collocations and practise the linking. In which collocations do you hear a /j/ sound?

1. absolutely everywhere
2. absolutely amazing
3. totally forgot
4. literally years
5. total disaster
6. absolute agony

4 Match the sentences 1–6 with the understatements a–f.

1. We don't see eye to eye on anything.
2. He is so old fashioned.
3. She's utterly obsessed with cats.
4. He's absolutely huge.
5. He revealed all the work gossip.
6. The project failed to meet the deadline.

a. He was a little indiscreet about his colleagues.
b. She's a bit of a cat lover.
c. He's slightly overweight at the moment.
d. He isn't exactly the most up-to-date man in the world.
e. We've got slightly different opinions.
f. It's a tiny bit late.

Extension

1 Rewrite the following sentences in a more exaggerated way.

1. It was hot in Majorca last week.
2. I haven't eaten all day.
3. It's a small house.
4. He's a good cook.

2 Write a dialogue containing the sentences above. Then record yourself saying them, paying particular attention to stress and intonation.

12 HOW TO USE *OH, AH, WOW, OUCH,* ETC.

About the language

> I've got to work this weekend.   Oh no. I thought we could have a day out.

There are a number of words – sometimes called *interjections* – that we use regularly in conversation, but hardly ever write down (so the spellings change sometimes). We say these words when we want to react positively or negatively to a situation. It is worth remembering that *Oh* is far more common than the rest.

1 *Oh*

Listen to three dialogues. Decide what *Oh* expresses in each one: surprise (S), disappointment (D) or understanding/realisation (U). Check your answers on page 53.

1   A: **Oh** dear. It looks like it's going to rain. Shall we just get a taxi?
    B: Yes, I suppose we'd better.
2   A: The problem is that my flat's too small.
    B: **Oh**, I see. Well, Sue can stay with me, if you like.
3   A: **Oh**, look at these flowers! Aren't they beautiful?
    B: Yes, they're lovely. Are they bluebells?

We often we use *oh* with *no* or with *yes/yeah*:

A: If you look between those two houses, you can see the sea.
B: **Oh yeah.** That's nice.

We also say *oh* before swear or taboo words and their more polite forms such as *Oh my goodness!*

Finally, we can use *oh* or *oh well* to change the subject of our conversation:

1   **Oh**, there's something else I wanted to ask. Will we need to book in advance?
2   **Oh well**, I think it's time for us to leave. It'll take half an hour to get to the station.

▶ Practice: Exercises 1, 2 and 3 pages 54–55.
▶ For the use of *oh* in reporting speech, see Unit 14, page 60.

2 *Ah, ooh, wow, aha, aah*

Look at the picture. When do you think we use *Aha*? Check your answers on page 49.

Aha! Now I know why you brought me here. It's where the actors come after the shows. You want to see how many stars you can spot.

Ah, *ooh* and *wow* also express surprise, but are a little stronger than *oh*. *Ah* and *ooh* can be positive or negative:

1   **Ah**, we're okay because there's a spare key above the door.
2   **Ooh**, it's freezing out here!

52

ABOUT THE LANGUAGE

A common meaning of *ah* is 'I've just had a good idea':

A: If our train's on time, we'll have three hours free in Edinburgh. Is there anything you want to see there? I don't really know the city myself.
B: **Ah** – why don't we speak to Amy? She was at college there, wasn't she?

Ooh often means 'I'll need time to think about that':

A: Why don't you come to Africa with me?
B: **Ooh**, that's an interesting idea.

Wow is normally positive:

A: Anyway, I decided to treat myself to a new dress. What do you think?
B: **Wow**! It's gorgeous.

Aha has a particular meaning: surprise when you suddenly understand something which you didn't understand before:

Aha! I know why we're leaving early. Carl wants to get home for the football match on TV.

By softly lengthening the vowel sound of *ah*, we make *aah*, which we use when we see or hear of something especially nice or cute:

Aah, look at that little baby monkey. Isn't it sweet?

▶ **Practice: Exercises 4 and 6 page 55.**

3 Oops, ouch, ow, yuk

All of these words express something negative. We say *oops* when we do or say something wrong:

Oops! I've just dropped some pasta on my trousers.

A: I think she'll be a great mum.
B: What do you mean?
A: **Oops**! She hasn't told you yet, has she?

Ouch and *ow* express pain. *Ouch* can sometimes mean mental rather than physical pain:

1 **Ow**! I've burnt myself!
2 **Ouch**! That's a cruel thing to say.

And *yuk* (also written as *euch*) expresses disgust:

Yuk! That tastes horrible.

A: ... and there was a mouse in my hotel room, too.
B: **Yuk**! How awful!

▶ **Practice: Exercises 5 and 6 page 55.**

Answers

1   1 D   2 U   3 S
2   When we suddenly understand something which we didn't understand before.

12 HOW TO USE OH, AH, WOW, OUCH, ETC.

Practice

1 Complete the dialogues with *Oh,* and a word in the box.

I'd • look • when • that's (x2) • do

1 **A:** Would you like a coffee?
  B: <u>Oh, I'd</u> love one, thanks

2 **A:** I got the job
  B: _____ fantastic! When do you start?

3 **A:** _____ at the snow, it's beautiful!
  B: Yes, but I'm glad I'm inside in the warm.

4 **A:** That dress looks really good on you.
  B: _____ you think so? Thanks.

5 **A:** Her father died last night.
  B: _____ terrible, is she okay?

6 **A:** I'm going travelling for a year.
  B: _____ did you decide that?

> When we use these words, we tend to say them louder and higher than normal.

2 Underline the correct alternatives to complete the dialogues.

1 **A:** If you right-click the mouse, that should fix it.
  B: *Oh yeah/Oh dear.* Thanks, it's working perfectly now.

2 **A:** They've had a flood in their flat. The living room's completely ruined.
  B: *Oh well/Oh no,* that's terrible!

3 **A:** *Oh my goodness/Oh yeah,* you've lost so much weight!
  B: Yes, I've been on a diet. I needed to lose a few kilos.

4 **A:** I couldn't come to the meeting as I was on the phone to a client.
  B: *Oh my goodness/Oh I see.* Well you didn't miss anything important.

5 **A:** Excuse me while I ring my doctor; I need to cancel an appointment.
  B: *Oh/Oh I see,* that reminds me: could you give me the name of your dentist?

3 Complete the telephone conversation with a suitable interjection.

Jess: Hello, Sam, it's Jess.
Sam: ¹ <u>Oh</u> Jess. I wasn't expecting to hear from you.
Jess: Listen, Nick says he can't go on holiday with us now, because of the cost.
Sam: ² _____! That messes everything up! Why has he suddenly changed his mind?
Jess: Well, he's just bought a flat and he says he has to save money now.
Sam: ³ _____, I see. Well, that's a shame – and a nuisance! But it does mean that we could invite Rudi instead, doesn't it?
Jess: ⁴ _____, that's true! I'll give him a ring!
Sam: Great. Let me know what he says.
Jess: Okay. ⁵ _____, I'd better go now. Speak soon.

4 Match statements 1–8 with responses a–h on page 55.

1 I've been head-hunted for a job in the US.
2 Let's go and see that horror film tonight.
3 What shall we do tonight?
4 Have a look at this photo of his kids.
5 Sue's leaving at the end of the month.
6 I've just booked a fortnight in Rio for £500.
7 You don't want dessert, do you?
8 I used to go out with that man over there.

PRACTICE

a Ah, I've had an idea, let's try that new club in town.
b Ooh, that could be good. I love a scare.
c Aah, twins, how lovely!
d Wow, that's amazing, well done. When do you start?
e Ooh, but that cake looks so nice …
f Aha, so that's why she's been so secretive lately.
g Aha, that's why he kept looking this way.
h Wow, you've got a really great deal.

5 Complete the sentences with *oops, ouch* or *yuk*.

1 **A:** There's a hair in my burger!
   B: _____! How horrible!
2 _____! That hurt. I caught my hand in the door!
3 _____! I've forgotten my wife's birthday.
4 **A:** Jack's slipped on the ice and broken his leg.
   B: _____! I bet that's painful!
5 _____! This milk's really sour. How old is it?
6 _____! The cat's scratched me again!
7 **A:** It'll be strange when Tim's gone to Germany.
   B: What?!
   A: _____! You don't know yet, do you?
8 **A:** _____! I think I've broken your camera.
   B: Don't worry. It's always doing that.

6a Four of the sentences/dialogues below contain the wrong interjections. Identify the mistakes and correct them.

1 Aha! Now I understand! You invited everyone to the surprise party while I was out last Saturday.
2 Oops – look at those little kids holding hands, they're so cute!
3 **A:** Shall we go and see that film?
   B: Yuk, I'm not sure. I'm not really in the mood for a serious drama.
4 Oops! So that's where she left the keys! I've been looking for them for days!
5 Wow! This place looks amazing! It must've taken you ages to decorate.
6 **A:** So how can we contact her?
   B: Ah! I know. She'll have her daughter's mobile phone with her.
7 Ouch, you bought me flowers! How romantic!
8 **A:** I've passed my driving test!
   B: Ow! First time, that's fantastic!

b Listen and check your answers. Then listen again and notice the intonation in the exclamations. Listen and repeat.

Extension

1 Imagine you are at a very luxurious party. Practise the conversation you might have with your friend about the food and drink you taste and the people and clothes that you see. Use some of the new words you have learnt in this unit.

2 What do you say in your own language in these situations?

1 when you are surprised by something
2 when you need time to think about something
3 when you suddenly understand something
4 when you do something wrong
5 when you feel sudden pain

55

13 MAKE STATEMENTS WORK AS QUESTIONS

About the language

| I've done all my e-mails. | Good. So you're ready to go? |

To make a statement into a question, we normally change the word order, or use *do/does/did* or a question tag. But it isn't always necessary. In spoken English, and perhaps in your language too, a statement such as *You're taking the early train* can become as a 'yes/no' question if you use it in the right place and with the right intonation or body language.

1 When to use statements as questions

Look at the two questions below. In what situations would you use them? Check your answers on page 57.

1 Did you speak to your boss?
2 You spoke to your boss, then?

The 'right place' to use a statement as a question is normally when both people already know what the conversation is about. For example, if a friend of yours starts talking about the beautiful Mexican countryside, you might reply: *Sounds wonderful. So you've been to Mexico recently?* On the other hand, if you simply want to find out if one of your friends knows the country, you'd probably start that bit of your conversation by using a 'full' question form such as: *Listen, have you ever been to Mexico?*

▶ **Practice: Exercise 1 page 58.**

2 Intonation

There is more than one way to pronounce a 'statement as question'. Intonation often depends on the meaning the person wants to express. We can, for example, be surprised or concerned; doubtful or certain; 'neutral' or careful – or we can use this structure to ask for clarification.

Listen to the intonation in the five conversations below, and decide what 'meaning' speaker B expresses in the questions. Check your answers on page 57.

1 **A:** Scott's booked a table for 6p.m.
  B: We're eating before the play?
  A: Yes, that's right.

2 **A:** Okay, we can go now.
  B: You've finished already? I thought that essay was going to take all day.

3 **A:** We'll pick Mike up on the way.
  B: Mike's coming, too?
  A: Yes, that's right. I hope that's okay. He's been feeling a bit lonely lately.

4 **A:** I saw this bottle of wine at £30.
  B: But you didn't buy it?
  A: What do you think?

5 **A:** I'm going out for a bit, I think.
  B: You'll take a coat? It's freezing.

▶ **Practice: Exercise 2 and 5 pages 58–59.**

It is quite common, particularly among younger people, to hear statements such as *I do a bit of yoga, because it helps me reduce stress.* that end with a rising intonation (↗) to express the idea 'Do you know what I mean?' or 'You agree with me, don't you?' These are a little different from statements as questions because they don't necessarily require a response.

ABOUT THE LANGUAGE

3 *So, then, but, and*

Quite often we start statements as questions with *so*, *but* or *and*. *So* means 'therefore' (as normal), and we sometimes replace it with *then* or add *then* to the end:

1 **A:** **So** we'll meet at the bank?
  B: That's right. About eleven.

2 **A:** I'm afraid I don't speak any Turkish.
  B: **So** you'll need a phrase book, **then**?

3 **A:** Actually, I'm free at from seven.
  B: **Then** you'll join us for lunch?

> " When we're expressing surprise, we sometimes repeat what we've heard as a question:
> **A:** *So I'm going to leave my job and set up a business.*
> **B:** *You're going to leave your job? Are you sure that's a good idea?*

4 **A:** You're a doctor, **then**?
  B: That's right. I qualified last year.

With *but* we are normally expressing a doubt or concern:

A: I'm not going to the first talk today.
B: Okay. **But** I'll see you later?
A: Sure, probably in the café.

We often use *and* to mean something like 'this is the way I hope it will be':

1 **A:** I'll send you my address when I get it.
  B: Good. **And** we'll stay in touch?
  A: Of course we will.

2 **A:** **And** you'll lock the door every time you go out?
  B: I said so, didn't I? You worry too much.

▶ **Practice: Exercises 3 page 59.**

Answers

1 Question 1 sounds like an 'open' question, where the speaker simply wants to find an answer. In question 2, the speaker seems to know already that their colleague has talked to their boss, and possibly wants to hear the outcome.

2 1 neutral 2 surprised 3 speaker B seems to be expressing some doubt about the idea that Mike is coming 4 speaker B seems sure that A didn't buy the wine 5 speaker B sounds worried/concerned

13 MAKE STATEMENTS WORK AS QUESTIONS

Practice

1 Match the sentences 1–8 to the responses a–h.

1 This is our tenth wedding anniversary.
2 I really miss working there.
3 He's nearly ready to leave.
4 I wonder what Tim's doing now.
5 It'll take ages to finish the art project.
6 I'll grab my discount railcard.
7 We've set the date.
8 The house is on the market.

a You lost touch with him?
b So they're actually moving?
c He's got his coat on?
d You're getting married?
e You'd like to go back, then?
f You've made a good start, though?
g So you plan to take the train?
h You actually remembered the date?

2 Listen to the underlined parts of the dialogues and decide if the speaker is expressing doubt (D), surprise (S) or if they are asking for clarification (C).

1 A: You saw Hilary?
   B: Yes, she came back for her mum's surprise birthday party.

2 A: I'll pick you up at six.
   B: You'll bring the car?
   A: Yes, I will.

3 A: I need to buy you some more chocolates.
   B: What! You've eaten them all?
   A: I'm afraid I couldn't resist!

4 A: I know you're in your new dress, but could you just check the oil in the car?
   B: You want me to do that?

5 A: The flight gets in at ten o'clock.
   B: So that's ten in the morning?
   A: That's right.

6 A: Your uncle's visiting tomorrow.
   B: For the whole weekend?
   A: For the whole week, actually!

3 Put the words into the correct order to make 'statements as questions'. Use capital letters and punctuation where necessary.

1 A: you're / then / so / Ruby's / boyfriend / new

   _____
   B: That's me!

2 A: you / the / so / at / I'll / station / see

   _____
   B: That's right. At ten thirty.

3 A: then / drive / you / so / don't?

   _____
   B: No, but I'm going to learn.

4 A: We're not going to LA now.
   B: still / in / but / meet / we'll / Toronto

   _____
   A: Sure.

5 A: I won't be here for Christmas.
   B: see / on / you / Eve / but / New / I'll / Year's

   _____
   A: Yes.

6 A: you'll / so / to / that / remember / post / card / birthday

   _____
   B: I'll do it on my way to work.

58

PRACTICE

4 **Matt's in Edinburgh and Chloe's in New York. They are talking on Skype. Complete the conversation with questions a–f below.**

Matt: At last, I've got through to you! It's been really difficult tonight.
Chloe: ¹_____ Sorry about that – I've been having connection problems my end.
Matt: Not to worry. Anyway, how are you? ²_____
Chloe: It's fine, though I do have something to tell you. I'm getting married next week.
Matt: *(pause)* What? ³_____ That's a bit of a shock. I didn't even know you were going out with anyone!
Chloe: Well, it's been a bit of a whirlwind romance – we met at a party last month, and it sort of developed from there.
Matt: My goodness. But hang on … ⁴_____
Chloe: No. It feels perfectly natural!
Matt: Hmm. Let me get this straight. ⁵_____
Chloe: Well, if you're going to be horrible …
Matt: Okay, okay, I'm sorry. I'm just really shocked, that's all.
Chloe: Look, don't worry. It won't affect anything, I promise.
Matt: Are you sure? ⁶_____
Chloe: We'll be fine. I'm actually hoping you'll come to the US for the wedding. You can meet Dave then, and you'll see how nice he is.

a You're getting married next week?!
b So next week you're marrying a man you hardly know, then?
c We'll still keep in touch? And it won't affect our friendship?
d You've been trying for a while?
e You don't think it's all a bit sudden?
f Everything okay in New York?

> *A whirlwind romance* is a love relationship that moves very fast.

Extension

1 **Finish the following statements as questions.**

1 So you've been to …?
2 We'll meet at …?
3 You're a … then?
4 But you didn't …?

2 **Prepare and practise some short dialogues using the sentences above, where one person needs to confirm something the other person says, or needs to express surprise or doubts. Use 'statements as questions' in your dialogues.**

3 **Record your dialogues, paying particular attention to stress and intonation.**

14 REPORT SPEECH IN A MORE IMMEDIATE WAY

About the language

> … but then she said, 'Oh, that's too expensive. You can't buy me that.'

Reporting speech normally involves a process of changing tenses, pronouns and time and place words. In this unit, we focus instead on a simpler way – and a special use of the past continuous.

1 Using direct speech

In conversation, we often want to tell friends about the things we or other people have said. If Holly says to Dave on a Saturday night: *I'm tired. I've had enough of this party*, he can tell a friend about it on Sunday, using the grammar of reported speech:

> Then Holly said she was tired and that she'd had enough of the party.

But he doesn't have to. It's easier and more natural in an informal context just to use Holly's actual words (direct speech):

> Then Holly said, 'I'm tired. I've had enough of this party.'

The only problem when we do this is that it's not always clear when our words end, and the direct speech begins. To solve this we sometimes use 'marker' words. These words, which may or may not have been used by the original speaker, act as speech marks.

(34) **Listen to the dialogue between work colleagues, and try to identify the three marker words that the speaker uses. Notice the stress they place on these words. Check your answers on page 61.**

> **Elsa:** I finally managed to get through to Tim on the phone today.
> **Jacob:** Good. How did it go?
> **Elsa:** Not very well. I started by saying to him, 'Look, if we don't find a way of working together, we'll never get the product launch ready in time.' And he said, 'Oh, I didn't know we had a problem.' So I said, 'Well, you haven't replied to any of my last three e-mails.'
> **Jacob:** And how did he respond?
> **Elsa:** He just told me to relax!

2 Seven marker words

The seven marker words that we sometimes use are: *but*, *hey*, *listen*, *look*, *oh*, *okay*, and *well*. As well as indicating when the direct speech begins, the one we choose can add drama to the report by revealing the attitude of the person who was speaking.

But, *listen* and *look* often introduce a different point of view:

> … and then Tom said to Sue, '**Listen**, I'm not your servant, you know.'
> She said to me, '**But** you can't go out dressed like that!'

Hey and *oh* sometimes express surprise:

> 1 Jane started to walk towards the door so Mark said, '**Hey**, where are you going?'
> 2 The shop assistant said it was only £10 and I said, '**Oh**, are you sure?'

Okay and *well* may suggest the speaker is hesitant or doubtful:

> … and I said, '**Okay**, you can have a shower, but we're going to be late again.'
> I didn't want to take my coat, but Bob said, '**Well**, it can be cold in Scotland.'

▶ Practice: Exercises 1–3 pages 62–63.

ABOUT THE LANGUAGE

3 Telling jokes and stories

When we tell a joke or a story, it's normal to use a 'direct' way of reporting speech.

Read this joke, and as you do so, try to find one other typical grammatical feature of storytelling. Then check your answers below.

Two men are going for a walk, when they see the fastest man-eating lion in the world in the distance. The first man takes a pair of running shoes out of his bag, and begins to put them on. The second man says to him, 'Hey, why are you doing that? You can't run faster than the world's fastest man-eating lion'. But the first man says, 'Listen, I only have to run faster than you'.

▶ Practice: Exercise 4 on page 63.

4 Using said, say(s), go(es) and went

In the examples so far in this unit, we've introduced speech with the past verb form *said*. But it is also possible, but only in **very informal** contexts to use the present tense *says*, or a past or present form of *go*:

1. Then after class yesterday, Becky **says** to me 'What are doing tonight?' and I **go**, 'I'm revising', and she **says**, 'You're always working, you. Why don't you take a break?'
2. Dave shouted at me again this morning, so I **went**, 'Look, why are you in such a bad mood these and he said, 'Sorry, I'm a bit stressed out about the exams next week.'

Young people in the UK, and people in TV dramas or soap operas, often use *be like*, but this is considered extremely informal, or incorrect by many people:

So then we had a bit of a row. Steve **is like**, 'You should have texted me if you weren't coming,' and **I'm like**, 'I told you already I'd forgotten to charge my mobile.'

5 Using the past continuous

We sometimes use *talk about* and *tell (someone) about* in the past continuous to introduce reports of recent conversations. Look at these examples:

1. Meg **was telling me about** her new dog yesterday. He's called Bruno and he's massive!
2. Ravi **was talking about** that new film with Johnny Depp. He says it's pretty good.
3. Anyway, I **was telling Chris about** my trip to Colombia, and he said he was planning to go there in the summer.

▶ Practice: Exercise 5 page 63.

Answers

1. look, oh, well.
2. It's also common in storytelling to use the present tense for dramatic effect.

14 REPORT SPEECH IN A MORE IMMEDIATE WAY

Practice

1a Lizzie and Sanjeet are complaining about their flatmates. Put the dialogue in the correct order.

- **a Lizzie:** That's typical of Mel. She's so rude and arrogant. She never lifts a finger and neither does Sophie. *And* she's been helping herself to my CDs. _____
- **b Sanjeet:** And what did she reply? _____
- **c Lizzie:** No, she's done it before. So I said to her, 'Look, just ask next time, will you?'
- **d Sanjeet:** I said to Mel, 'Look, why don't you ever do any washing up?' and she said 'Listen, I'm hardly ever here. Why should I?' _1_
- **e Lizzie:** She just said, 'Oh, I didn't think you'd mind.' Honestly, it drives you mad! I can't wait till we find a new flat.
- **f Sanjeet:** She hasn't, has she? Is it the first time?

(35) **b** Listen to check your answers. Then listen and repeat, paying attention to stress.

2 Kate is talking to a friend on the phone. Complete what she says with the actual words she used a–e.

So I phoned John and said, 'What time do you think you can meet?' And he said, '1_____' So I said, '2_____' And do you know how long I was waiting? An hour and a half! Then when he finally turned up, I really shouted at him. I said, '3_____' He didn't even say he was sorry. He just turned round and said, '4_____' I could have killed him, you know. But in the end, I just went '5_____' and I just came home.

- a Hey, calm down! It's not the end of the world!
- b Who do you think you are, making me wait like this?
- c Well actually it is– I'm not in the mood now.
- d Well, I should be able to get to the restaurant by 7p.m.
- e That sounds great.

> "Marker words always come at the beginning of the utterance and are always stressed!"

3a Put the words in brackets in the correct order to complete these sentences.

1. I said, (up? / hurry / Look, / you / will) '_____ I don't want to miss the start of the film.'
2. So I said, (keep / will you? / shouting, / don't / Listen,) '_____ I don't want the whole street to hear us arguing.'
3. Hilary said, (you can / than 20kg. / Well, I / carry more / don't think) '_____ They'll charge you for excess weight at check-in.'
4. I said, (more sweets. / have some / Okay, / you can) '_____ But don't blame me if you're sick.'
5. So I said, (you / what / are / here? / doing / Hey,) '_____? You should be at school!'
6. And then I said, (don't think / the right change / given me / you've / Oh, I) '_____.I gave you a *ten* pound note.'

b Match the sentences 1–6 above with the responses a–f.

- a So did he stop eating then?
- b Did you get there on time in the end?
- c So did you manage to have a proper conversation after that?
- d And did he have a good excuse for being out of school?
- e Hmm, I think she's right about the 20kg limit.
- f So did you get the right change in the end?

PRACTICE

4 Put the words in brackets in the correct place to complete the joke.

A bank robber goes to prison for stealing, but he *refuses* to tell the police where he's hidden the money. His wife telephones him in prison and, 'Darling, I need to plant the potatoes now. I suppose I'll have to do dig the garden myself this year.' The robber replies, 'don't touch the garden! That's where I buried the money!'
A week later he's having his lunch and he another phone call from his wife, saying, 'you won't believe this, but yesterday seven policemen came to the house and dug up the garden! They didn't seem happy.' The robber for a minute or two, and then says to his wife, 'now plant the potatoes!'

[refuses]

[says]

[Hey,]
[gets]
[Listen,]

[laughs]
[Okay,]

5 Complete the dialogues with the words in the box.

You've • Look • said • talking • telling • saying • having

Kay: I was ¹_____ a chat with Sal this morning. She was ²_____ me about her new flat. It sounds really nice. Really spacious. What about you? Have you had a good day?

Jo: Actually, no. I had a horrible lunch date with that guy, Phil. He just kept staring at me, and then he said, '³_____ got really beautiful eyes, Jo.' That's a bit strange, isn't it? So I just said, 'Oh, thank you!' Anyway, after that it got worse, because when the bill came he said, '⁴_____ I'm sorry, but I've left my wallet at home' – and he'd promised to pay!

* * *

Sean: Dan was ⁵_____ about that bomb scare at the station.
Kieran: Really? What was he ⁶_____?
Sean: Well, apparently, a man's voice came over the loudspeaker and just ⁷_____, 'This is an emergency, please leave the station immediately.'

Extension

Choose some of the topics below, and write them down using reported speech. Then record your piece. Make the intonation as dramatic as possible.

1 Report a real conversation you had yesterday.
2 Tell a joke.
3 Describe a complaint you made in a restaurant.
4 Describe an argument you had with an old friend or family member.
5 Describe a bad experience in a shop.
6 Describe a conversation that shocked or amazed you.

15 USE *HAD BETTER, HAVE GOT TO* AND *BE SUPPOSED TO* CORRECTLY

About the language

> **You'd better** hurry, Sue. **Aren't you supposed to** be meeting Chris at seven?

Three modal verb phrases, which you will have seen before, are much more common in conversation than in written English: *had better, have got to* and *be supposed to*. The purpose of this unit is to bring them together and check that you understand their meaning, form and pronunciation.

1 Comparing the three verb phrases

Listen to a conversation between Kevin and Sara and answer the questions. Then check your answers on page 65.

> 1 Why is Kevin surprised to see Sara?
> 2 Why couldn't Sara stay at work?
> 3 What is the aim of Sara's presentation?

Listen again and read the text, paying attention to the pronunciation of the three verb phrases.

> Kevin: **Aren't** you **supposed to** be at work?
> Sara: It's okay. My boss gave me the afternoon off. I**'ve got to** do a presentation tomorrow for some clients. The phone was ringing all the time, so she said I**'d better** go home and finish it off there.
> Kevin: You**'ve got to** use PowerPoint and all that, have you?
> Sara: If it helps, yes. I**'m supposed to** get our visitors to double their order with us.
> Kevin: That's tough. You**'d better** get on with it then, I suppose. I'll make us some dinner.

Which phrase is closest in meaning to *must*? Which is similar to *expect*? Which offers strong advice? Check your answers on page 65.

2 *Had better*

The meaning of *had better* is something like 'Here is my advice and if you don't take it, there will probably be a negative result.' After *had better*, we use an infinitive without *to*, and sometimes a question tag:

> You**'d better** get some sleep, hadn't you? You've got an important exam tomorrow.

Had better has a negative form:

> We**'d better not** buy anything else, or we'll have a huge credit card bill this month!

The question form is usually negative too:

> **Hadn't** we **better** leave? It's getting late.

In spoken English *had* is normally pronounced 'd, as in the examples above, or it disappears:

> You **better** be careful with that plate. It's really hot.

Note that we don't use *had better* to talk about the past, or to recommend things:

> ~~You'd better~~ see the new Picasso exhibition!

Use something like *You really must* ... instead.

▶ Practice: Exercises 1 and 2 page 66.

ABOUT THE LANGUAGE

3 Have got to

Have got to has the same meaning as *have to*, but it is much more common in spoken English, particularly in its present positive form. In written English, it tends to express 'external' obligation and *must* expresses 'internal' or 'personal' obligation:

1 I've **got to** submit this essay by 6p.m.on Friday.
2 We **must** try and keep in touch.

In spoken English *have got to* is also used for internal obligation, making it sound stronger:

I've **got to** do something about my hair. It's a mess.

Have got to has a negative and a question form:

1 We **haven't got to** pay now, have we?
2 **Have** we **got to** change trains at Paris?

It does not have a future form (*I'll have got to*), although we regularly use the present form to talk about future events:

I**'ve got to** go to the hospital on Friday.

In spoken English, *have got to* is normally pronounced *'ve got to* or *got to* or *gotta*:

1 They **got to** get their visas before they can travel.
2 You **gotta** see these photos. They're amazing!

▶ Practice: Exercise 3 page 67.

4 Be supposed to

We use *be supposed to* for things we 'expect' to happen:

1 Carlos **is supposed to** be here by now. Do you think he's got lost?
2 You're **supposed to** take your shoes off before you enter the temple. (It's a rule that you're expected to follow.)

Negative, question and past forms are common:

1 You're **not**/You **aren't supposed to** park here.
2 **Are** we **supposed to** take a gift with us?
3 I **was supposed to** meet her at the station, but I forgot. She's pretty mad at me.

The continuous form is also common, and it often carries a negative meaning:

I'**m supposed to** be making tonight's dinner. (But I'm not sure if I want to.)

In spoken English, the 'u' sound of 'supposed' disappears, and the second part of the word sounds like 'post' as in 'post a letter': *s'post*.

▶ Practice: Exercise 4 page 67.

Answers

1   1 He's surprised because she's supposed to be at work.   2 There were too many distractions, such as the phone ringing.   3 She's supposed to get the visitors to double their order.

2   must– *have got to*; expect – *be supposed to*; strong advice – *had better*

15 USE HAD BETTER, HAVE GOT TO AND BE SUPPOSED TO CORRECTLY

Practice

1a Match 1–8 with a–h to complete the statements.

1 You'd better pick up your prescription.
2 You'd better get going now, hadn't you?
3 He'd better hurry up
4 You'd better not touch that cut on your arm
5 She'd better not say anything about the party.
6 We'd better go to the supermarket, hadn't we?
7 You'd better not have another coffee.
8 You'd better post that card on the way to work.

a or I'll go without him.
b There's no food in the cupboards.
c I'll be really angry if she ruins the surprise.
d You're meeting her at five and its ten to now.
e The chemist shuts at five.
f or it might get infected.
g It's her birthday tomorrow.
h You won't be able to sleep tonight.

b Listen to check your answers. Notice how *had* is pronounced. Listen again and repeat.

2 Look at the texts 1–6 and then match them with replies a–f.

1 Missed the last train!
2 Just popping to atm
3 Ed asked me out!
4 What should I bring?
5 U still up?
6 Lost my key!

a You'd better bring walking boots – we'll be covering about fifteen miles a day
b U sure? Isn't there one at 12.45?
c You'd better get enough cash for tonight – club'll be expensive
d Am, but'd better get some sleep. Got early start tomorrow!
e Better not tell Adam, he's v jealous!
f Better leave mine out for u then, eh? It'll be under doormat!

3a Put the words in the correct order to make sentences. Add punctuation where necessary.

1 family / a / we've / to / got / to / go / reunion

2 to / the / got / I've / go / dentist / to

3 see / got / my / to / new / you've / car

4 weight / lose / got / to / I've

5 smoking / he's / to / stop / got

6 restaurant / you've / try / got / to / that / Indian / new

PRACTICE

b Complete 1–6 with the sentences in Exercise 3a on page 66.

1 _____, this tooth's really hurting again.
2 _____. The food's amazing.
3 **A:** _____! **B:** New car? What is it?
4 _____ – he's got the most awful cough these days.
5 **A:** What're you up to at the weekend?
   B: _____ for my nan's 90th birthday.
6 _____ – I can't fit into any of my clothes anymore.

b Listen to check your answers. Listen again and make a note of whether you hear 've got to or got to.

4 Complete the student dialogues 1–6 with phrases a–f.

1 **A:** This is strange!
   B: What is?
   A: Well, _____ start now, but there's nobody here.

2 **A:** (on the phone) Where are you?
   B: At home.
   A: Well, _____ for a seminar.
   B: Oh no!

3 **A:** This new class is early. I mean, _____ 8.30?
   B: Well, that's what the timetable says.

4 **A:** What are you up to later?
   B: _____ with Matt.
   A: Well, there's a party in the student bar.

5 **A:** Listen, _____ a presentation?
   B: Yeah. Apparently we've got five minutes each to describe our projects.

6 **A:** Hey, you can't hand in that assignment.
   B: Why not?
   A: Well, _____ write it by hand, it needs to be typed.

a you're not supposed to
b I'm supposed to be out
c you're supposed to be here
d is it supposed to start at
e the lecture's supposed to
f are we supposed to give

5 Complete the following monologues with the correct form of *had better*, *have got to* and *be supposed to*;

(company director, addressing employees)
Thanks for coming everyone. I'm sorry I've had to call you all to this meeting at such short notice, but I thought I ¹_____ let you know what's going on. As I'm sure you're all aware, the company has been in difficulty for some time now. What with the global recession and more recently, the changes in government, I'm afraid we ² _____ think about making cuts. I'm not ³_____ speak so candidly until things have been finalised, but I feel we owe you this much as long-standing employees of the company.

(two colleagues after the meeting)
Are we ⁴_____ just sit here and let the management walk all over us? No! We ⁵ _____ fight this all the way! We ⁶_____ organise ourselves and work out a plan of action!!

Extension

Imagine you have to show a new student/employee around your school/workplace. What kinds of things would you need to tell them? (e.g. rules, obligations, some advice.)
Prepare a monologue as you guide the person around.

16 MAKE SHORT RESPONSES TO AGREE OR SHOW INTEREST

About the language

> I'll see you tonight, then.   Great. Lovely.
>
> **The way in which we respond to what people say is one of the most important parts of conversational English. In this unit, we look at using adjectives, adverbs and very short questions. (See also Units 6, 12, and 18 for other ways of responding.)**

1 Response adjectives

Look at the dialogue below. If you had to put two words in front of *fine* to make a short sentence, what would they be? Check your answers on page 69.

> **A:** ... and I've made plenty of non-meat dishes too, for any vegetarians.
> **B:** Fine. Thanks very much.

When we are happy with a plan or a service, it's natural to respond with a positive adjective such as *fine, good, great, lovely, perfect*. We can also use the slightly stronger adjectives *brilliant, excellent, fantastic, wonderful*.

(39) **Listen and repeat. Notice the intonation the speakers use in the responses to agree or show interest.**

> 1 **A:** We can have a pizza before the film.
>   **B:** **Great.**
>
> 2 **A:** Tim's coming to the match.
>   **B:** **Excellent.** I haven't seen him for ages.
>
> 3 **A:** (*at a hotel*) I've booked you a taxi, madam, and here's a map of the city centre.
>   **B:** **Fantastic.** Thank you very much.

Sometimes we use more than one adjective – to add to our satisfaction or to show that the arrangement is complete:

> **A:** (*at a conference*) ... and you can use the computers in the business centre.
> **B:** **Brilliant. Perfect.** I'll check my e-mail straight away, if I may.

▶ Practice: Exercise 1 page 70.

2 Response adverbs

We often use the adverbs *absolutely*, *definitely* and *certainly* (with or without *yes/yeah*) to show that we agree with something.

(40) **Listen to the dialogues below. How is *certainly* is a little different from *absolutely* and *definitely*? Check your answers on page 69.**

> 1 **A:** Do you think he'll like this CD?
>   **B:** **Absolutely.**
>
> 2 **A:** I think Rome's a great city.
>   **B:** Yeah, **definitely**.
>
> 3 **A:** Can I borrow your dictionary?
>   **B:** **Certainly.**
>
> 4 **A:** Could I have a glass of water?
>   **B:** Yes, **certainly**.

ABOUT THE LANGUAGE

We normally add *not* when we reply to negative statements/questions:

1 **A:** They shouldn't make you pay everything in advance.
  B: Absolutely not.

2 **A:** You didn't leave your wallet at Annie's, did you?
  B: Definitely not.

▶ Practice: Exercises 2 and 3 page 70.

3 Response questions

Look at the dialogues below. Why does the person responding use *Has* in the first, and *Did* in the second? Check your answers below.

1 **A:** Diana's left her job.
  B: Has she? That's brave.

2 **A:** I went to the match yesterday.
  B: Did you?

Response questions are short forms of regular questions. They're a good way of showing interest and continuing conversations. We sometimes add *oh* and *really*.

🔊 (41) **Listen and notice the intonation, and the fact that negative statements need negative questions.**

1 **A:** Di and Rod have bought a flat in Spain.
  B: Have they really?
  A: Yeah. It's near Barcelona.

2 **A:** Sheila's ill today, I'm afraid.
  B: Oh is she?
  A: Yes. I think she's got flu.

3 **A:** I couldn't find a dress in my size.
  B: Couldn't you?
  A: No. They'd sold out.

4 **A:** He doesn't like spicy food.
  B: Oh, doesn't he?

▶ Practice: Exercise 4 page 71.

4 Showing strong surprise

To express strong surprise, we use *did* + *what*, after our partner has used the past simple:

  A: He got up and left half way through dinner.
  B: He **did what**?

Did + *what* after the past simple is the commonest form, but other tenses are possible:

  A: I've just bought a motorbike.
  B: You've **done what**?

▶ Practice: Exercise 5 on page 71.

Answers

1 You could say *That's fine.* or *That sounds fine.*
2 *Certainly* is a little weaker and we normally use it (or *Of course*) to reply automatically to requests.
3 They work like questions: if there is *have* or *be* or a modal verb, you can use it; if there isn't, then you use a form of *do*.

69

16 MAKE SHORT RESPONSES TO AGREE OR SHOW INTEREST

Practice

1 Complete the adjectives in the responses.

1. **A:** We've got time for a coffee before the show.
   B: L_____.
2. **A:** I've brought a takeaway!
   B: Br_____!
3. **A:** The weather's looking good for our picnic.
   B: P_____.
4. **A:** Paul's going to call before he goes to Egypt.
   B: G_____.
5. **A:** I've actually passed my driving test!
   B: F_____!
6. **A:** I've got tickets for the Picasso exhibition.
   B: W_____.

2 Solve the anagrams in brackets for the correct responses.

1. **A:** Could you pass the salt?
   B: _____. (yrlcraetni)
2. **A:** What a beautiful sunset!
   B: _____. (esayllbuot)
3. **A:** London's a fascinating city, isn't it?
   B: _____. (hyae, eiydlfitne)
4. **A:** Are you sure you don't want to go to the party?
   B: _____. (yosleaubtl otn)
5. **A:** What we've just eaten shouldn't cost this much.
   B: _____. (ndifeylit ont)

3 <u>Underline</u> the correct alternative.

1. **A:** Have you had enough to eat?
   B: *Good./Absolutely.* I'm full.
2. **A:** Could you tell me the time?
   B: *Certainly./Wonderful.*
3. **A:** You didn't forget to pack your swimming costume, did you?
   B: *Absolutely not./Lovely.*
4. **A:** Here's your birthday present.
   B: *Brilliant, thanks. /Yeah definitely, thanks.*
5. **A:** Can I come over at nine o'clock?
   B: *Definitely not, see you then!/Certainly, see you then!*
6. **A:** I thought we could see a show.
   B: *Great!/Absolutely not!* I'd love that.

4 Complete the dialogues on page 71 with a response from box A and the final reply from box B.

A

Oh, are you? • Has it? • Couldn't you? • Oh, aren't they? • ~~Oh, did you?~~ • Has she really?

B

I'm afraid so. I shouldn't have eaten that last cream cake.
Yes. She just couldn't rely on him.
Yes, and I bought a new battery only a week ago.
No. My dad's knees are bad, and my mum's got flu.
No. I was sure I was going to fail the course.
~~Yes, I'm afraid so. The property market is so bad at the moment.~~

PRACTICE

1 **A:** I sold my flat for less than I paid for it!
   B: *Oh, did you?*
   A: *Yes, I'm afraid so. The property market is so bad at the moment.*

2 **A:** My watch has stopped.
   B: _____
   A: _____

3 **A:** I'm feeling sick!
   B: _____
   A: _____

4 **A:** I couldn't sleep for worrying!
   B: _____
   A: _____

5 **A:** Jo told me she's left her boyfriend.
   B: _____
   A: _____

6 **A:** My parents aren't well enough to travel.
   B: _____
   A: _____

5a Complete the dialogue with Ray's shocked responses.

Pat: Ralph went flying last weekend.
Ray: ¹ *He did what?*
Pat: Well, I gave him flying lessons for his sixtieth birthday.
Ray: ² _____?
Pat: Anyway, he'd been doing well, so he and his wife decided to hire a light plane and fly across to France!
Ray: ³ _____?
Pat: Unfortunately, they got into trouble coming back over the English Channel. Ralph fainted, actually.
Ray: ⁴ _____?
Pat: So his wife made an emergency landing in a field in Kent!
Ray: ⁵ _____?
Pat: And then she had to revive him.
Ray: ⁶ _____?
Pat: So it was all okay in the end! You can't stop doing things when you get older, you know.

b Listen and mark the stress and intonation in Ray's responses.

Extension

Look at these situations and think about when you would show agreement, interest or shock. What would your actual words be? Write short dialogues for each situation.

1 Someone has bought you a surprise present.
2 A friend asks if you would write her a job reference.
3 You hear that your cousin has won a big prize in the lottery.
4 A friend asks if you would lend her £500.
5 Your brother says he is very sorry, but he can't drive you to the airport.

17 ADD VERB, ADVERB AND ADJECTIVE PAIRS

About the language

> You've got to take a break now and then, haven't you?

In conversation we sometimes like to use verbs, adverbs and adjectives in pairs, linked by *and*. With verbs and adverbs, it adds a sense of action and movement; with adjectives, it adds emphasis to a description. In this unit, we look at some common pairs.

1 Verb pairs

Apart from a few expressions like *wait and see*, the most frequent pairs start with *go*, *come* and *try*. We normally use them as infinitives, often after *can/could/be going to/will/shall/let's/why don't (you/we*, etc.) or as imperatives in requests, e.g. *Come and sit here.*

go + and + ask/buy/do/find/have/get/look/see/sit/take (a look)
We often use the phrases above when we're discussing plans with friends and family:

1 Why don't you **go and ask** that man what time the museum closes?
2 I'm going to **go and do** some shopping.
3 Ask Dave to **go and find** a map.
4 Shall we **go and have** a coffee?
5 **Go and look** for them – it's time to leave.
6 Could you **go and see** if they give a student discount?
7 Is the café still open? Shall we **go and take** a look?

> There is a fixed pattern with the present perfect form of *go + and +* past participle that we sometimes use to criticise someone's behaviour:
> He's gone and eaten all the cakes you made.
> I've gone and said the wrong thing, haven't I?

🔊(43) **Listen to the sentences above. How are the words *go and* pronounced? Can you hear a sound between *go* and *and*? How is the word *and* itself pronounced? Check your answers on page 73.**

come + and + get/have/help/ look/say/see/sit/stay/tell
We often use the phrases above when we're asking people to do things:

1 Are you going to **come and get** this food while it's hot?
2 **Come and have** a word with Kate. She doesn't know what to do.
3 **Come and look** at this dog!
4 Do **come and see** me when you're in Paris.
5 **Come and sit** next to me.
6 You can **come and stay** with us whenever you like.

try + and + do/find/get/make/put/remember
We often use the phrases above to make requests and suggestions:

1 **Try and do** some tidying while we're out. It's your turn.
2 Shall we **try and find** that restaurant we liked last year?
3 I know you don't enjoy parties, but will you **try and make** an effort tonight?
4 **Try and remember** when you last used your wallet.

▶ Practice: Exercises 1, 2, 3 and 6 pages 74–75.

2 Adjective pairs

What are the missing adjectives in the examples below? Check your answers on page 73.

1 I'm sick and _____ of studying!
2 You don't have to shout. I can hear you _____ and clear.

We often use adjectives in pairs for emphasis:

1 It's **cold and wet** outside again.
2 What a **weird and wonderful** little museum!

72

ABOUT THE LANGUAGE

Other common pairs are: *soft and smooth, bright and early, rich and famous, tall and handsome, hot and stuffy, old and frail*. All of the pairs above are 'fixed' as idioms, so we don't normally change the order – but you'll see some examples in the exercises that are more inventive, and where the order is 'freer'.

A second category of adjective pair is when we say how satisfied we are with something. These pairs normally start with *nice* or *lovely* – but it's the second adjective which actually expresses the meaning.

1 This room is **nice and warm**, isn't it?
2 It's great here! All the shops are **nice and close**.
3 Come and get this food while it's **lovely and hot**.
4 Get up! It's **lovely and sunny** outside.

We also use *good* with 'practical' things:

1 This bag of yours is **good and strong**.
2 Bring your bike. The roads round here are **good and flat**.

▶ Practice: Exercises 3, 4 and 6 pages 74–75.

3 Adverb pairs

The adverb pairs in bold in the examples below are all fairly common in conversation:

1 He makes the same mistake **again and again**. What can we do?
2 I've been running **back and forth/backwards and forwards** all day. I'm exhausted.
3 You should have fixed the car **there and then**. It's risky to drive around with it like that.
4 It's been raining **on and off** most of the day, so I haven't felt like going out.
5 We went **up and down** the street several times, but we couldn't find the shop you mentioned.
6 There are a few mistakes **here and there**, but it's a good essay in general.
7 I try to read a novel **now and again/now and then**, but I don't have much time.

8 It's been difficult to get my work done. The decorators have been coming **in and out** all day.

▶ Practice: Exercises 5 and 6 page 75.

Answers

1 You can normally hear /w/ between *go* and *and*, making pronunciation easier. The /a/ in *and* is unstressed and pronounced as /ə/, the sound known as 'schwa'. This pronunciation of and is normal in all verb, adjective and adverb pairs.
2 1 sick and *tired* 2 *loud* and clear

73

17 ADD VERB, ADVERB AND ADJECTIVE PAIRS

Practice

1a Complete the sentences with the phrases in the box.

> you're sorry • at this website • her computer • this great band • somewhere else to stay • turns up • you put my keys • in the new place

1 Can you try and remember where _____. I can't find them!
2 Come and see _____ with me. They're called the Cesarians.
3 Go and tell her that _____. It'll mean a lot to her.
4 We're finished! I want you to go and find _____.
5 You're good with technology; why don't you go and help her with _____?
6 Come and stay with us as soon as we get settled _____.
7 Come and look _____.
8 I'll just wait and see if he _____.

b Match the sentences 1–8 above with the responses a–h.

a You can find any book that's ever been published.
b Fine! I don't want to stay here any longer anyway!
c I think you're wasting your time. You've been stood up!
d Oh okay, but I don't see why *I* should apologise. She's the one who's in the wrong.
e Have you tried looking in the kitchen, on the fridge?
f Yeah, okay. Where are they playing?
g I'd like that. I can't wait to see the house.
h Me? You must be joking. I'm awful with computers!

> *To stand somebody up* means 'not to meet somebody you have arranged to meet', used especially for a romantic date.

(44) 2 Listen and note the sound you hear between the underlined words. Then listen and repeat.

1 <u>Go and</u> tell her that you're sorry.
2 I want you to <u>go and</u> find somewhere else to stay.
3 <u>Try and</u> finish work early tonight.
4 <u>Go and</u> help her with her computer.
5 <u>Go and</u> have a bath.
6 Can you <u>try and</u> meet the deadline.
7 <u>Go and</u> put the kettle on!
8 Will you <u>try and</u> put me on the guest list?
9 <u>Go and</u> tidy your room!
10 Could you <u>try and</u> find the phone bill?

3a Solve the anagrams in brackets to complete the pairs of positive adjectives.

1 loud and _clear_ (aelcr)
2 rich and _____ (safomu)
3 warm and _____ (lirfendy)
4 tall and _____ (hdsanmoe)
5 bright and _____ (yalre)
6 soft and _____ (omosth)

b Complete the sentences with the adjective pairs above.

1 **A:** Her boyfriend's gorgeous!
   B: He might be _____, but he's not very intelligent.
2 I wish I had hair like hers, it always looks so _____.
3 You don't have to shout, I can hear you _____!
4 The party was great. The atmosphere was so _____.
5 Why does everyone want to be _____?
6 They like to get up _____ every day.

PRACTICE

4a Match 1–6 to a–f to complete the sentences.

1 It's really hot and stuffy in here.
2 I'm sick and tired
3 It's so cold and wet outside.
4 She's getting a bit old and frail
5 He looks so sad and lonely.
6 It's a weird and wonderful shop

a now that she's in her eighties.
b that sells all sorts of strange old things.
c I feel sorry for him.
d Can you open the window?
e Let's just stay in and watch a DVD.
f of all this paperwork!

b Listen to check your answers. Then listen again and repeat the phrases, focusing on the stress and making sure you use the weak (schwa /ə/) form of *and*.

5 Make six common pairs from the adverbs in the box. Then complete the dialogues.

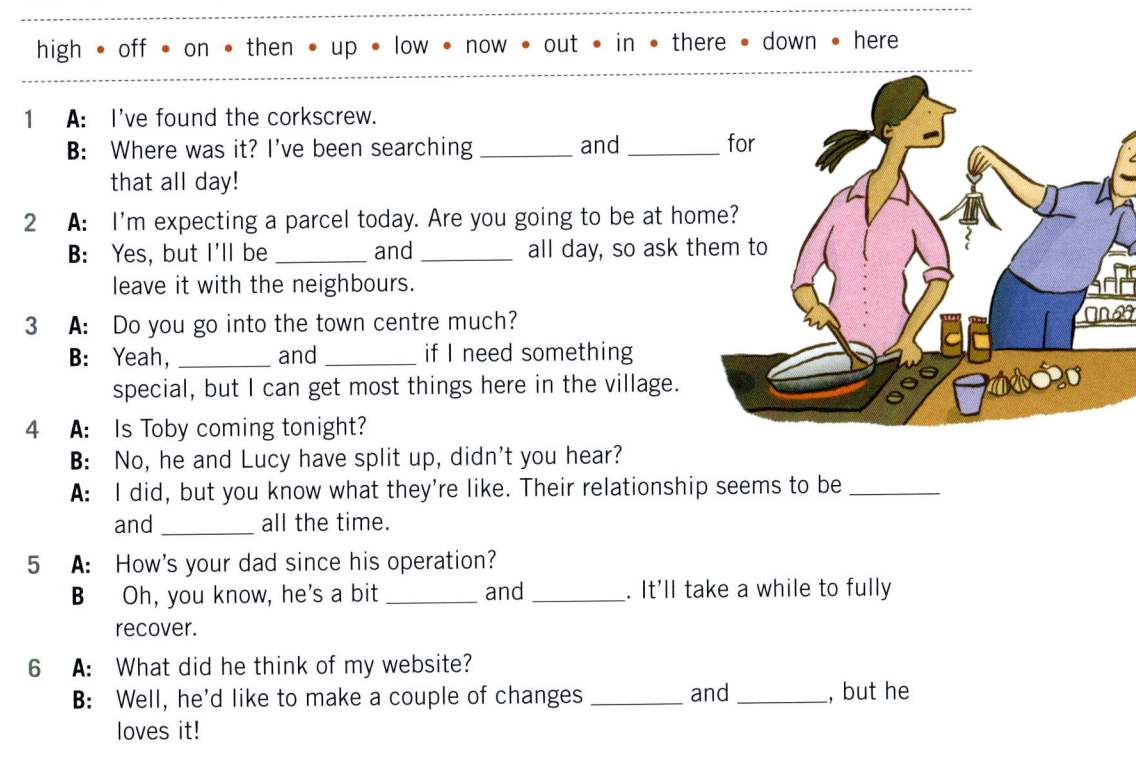

---
high • off • on • then • up • low • now • out • in • there • down • here
---

1 **A:** I've found the corkscrew.
   B: Where was it? I've been searching _____ and _____ for that all day!
2 **A:** I'm expecting a parcel today. Are you going to be at home?
   B: Yes, but I'll be _____ and _____ all day, so ask them to leave it with the neighbours.
3 **A:** Do you go into the town centre much?
   B: Yeah, _____ and _____ if I need something special, but I can get most things here in the village.
4 **A:** Is Toby coming tonight?
   B: No, he and Lucy have split up, didn't you hear?
   A: I did, but you know what they're like. Their relationship seems to be _____ and _____ all the time.
5 **A:** How's your dad since his operation?
   B Oh, you know, he's a bit _____ and _____. It'll take a while to fully recover.
6 **A:** What did he think of my website?
   B: Well, he'd like to make a couple of changes _____ and _____, but he loves it!

6 Complete the Skype chat from Sydney to London with an adjective or adverb from the box.

---
hot • see • down • clear • lively • visit • get • join • wet • crackly
---

Milos: Hello, can you hear me? It's really horrible and ¹_____ at my end …
Pedro: I can hear you loud and ²_____! Happy New year!
Milos: And to you! Wow, that looks like a great party you're having.
Pedro: Yeah, everyone's here. We wish you could come and ³_____ us.
Milos: It would be great, wouldn't it? How's London?
Pedro: Oh, the usual cold and ⁴_____ weather, but it's a great party here – a really good and ⁵_____ atmosphere. How's it going down under?
Milos: Well, my lifestyle's great – the weather's lovely and ⁶_____, I've got a great job. But I do miss my friends from London. Talking of which, when are you and Lara going to come and ⁷_____?
Pedro: Not sure actually. Things have been a bit up and ⁸_____ with my job and other stuff this year, so we'll have to wait and ⁹_____. Hey, here's Sue – she's dying to say 'Hi'. I'm going to go and ¹⁰_____ another drink, so I'll see you later.

> *Down under* means Australia to British people – because it is in the southern hemisphere.

Extension

Imagine you and a friend have just had a disappointing evening out at a restaurant. Brainstorm some possible ideas of what was wrong. Write the conversation you and your friend have on the way home from the restaurant. Record your conversation. Pay particular attention to stress and linking.

75

18 FOLLOW YOUR PARTNER

About the language

> It's a great view! Magic, isn't it?

Conversation, unlike writing, is interactive. People have the chance to build a conversation together, checking meaning, showing interest, pushing things forward. You've probably heard someone finishing someone else's words, for example, to help the other person – or sometimes out of impatience! In this unit, we'll look at ways in which people link what they say directly to the sentence they've just heard in a conversation.

1 Using an adjective with a similar meaning

Underline the adjective that B uses to 'repeat' what A has said in the dialogues below, as in the example. Check your answers on page 77.

> A: It's hot today isn't it
> B: Boiling! Shall we sit in the garden?

> 1 A: They shouldn't keep people waiting like this. It's terrible.
> B: You're right. It's awful.

> 2 A: I'm full. That was a beautiful meal.
> B: Gorgeous, wasn't it? Do you want some coffee?

> 3 A: This dress is fantastic, isn't it?
> B: Let's have a look. Oh, yes. It's stunning!

In our replies, particularly when someone is describing something, we often use adjectives with a similar meaning to show agreement, or just to fill a space until we've got something new to say. We may use the adjective immediately on its own (as in the first example above), or with a question tag (as in the third example). Or we might use it later on, after *it's*. Sometimes, in fact, a single word is enough as a reply:

> A: It's cold out here.   B: Freezing!

▶ Practice: Exercise 1 page 78.

2 Using a phrase with a similar meaning

In these examples, B uses a phrase rather than a single word to repeat what A has said.

> 1 A: He's got some interesting things to say, but he just keeps talking!
> B: You're right. **He never stops**.

> 2 A: It's really busy here, isn't it?
> B: Yes, **there's quite a crowd**. Shall we try to find some space?

What sort of phrases could B use in the gap below to 'repeat' what A has said? Check your answers on page 77.

> A: Carla is still studying at midnight most days.
> B: I know. She _____.

ABOUT THE LANGUAGE

Note how we often indicate our agreement first, with *Yes* or a phrase like *You're right* or *I know* or, as the example below, *That's true*:

> **A:** Have you noticed the way Mike never gives you a straight answer when you ask him if he wants to do something?
> **B:** That's true. **He's always keeping his options open**.

▶ Practice: Exercise 2 page 78.

3 Adding a dependent clause

Another way of linking your sentence to a previous one is to 'add' a dependent clause. *Which* and *because* clauses are sometimes used in this way.

> **A:** I've got some good news. I got that job I applied for.
> **B:** Which explains why there's a bottle of champagne in the fridge.
> **A:** Exactly. Shall we open it?

Underline the 'added' clauses in the dialogues below. You can add to your own previous sentence, as well as someone else's. Check your answers below.

1. **A:** Anyway, I spent ages helping him with his project, but he didn't give me a word of thanks.
   B: Really?
   A: Which is rude, isn't it?

2. **A:** I've bought lots of stuff from the market.
   B: I can see.
   A: 'Cos I'm going to try that Thai recipe from the internet.

3. **A:** I don't feel that good.
   B: Because you've been sitting in front of that computer all day.
   A: I suppose so. I'd better go for a run or something.

We can also add *if/unless* clauses:

1. **A:** This steak will be delicious.
   B: **If you don't burn it**. Be careful.

2. **A:** Steve's got to win the prize this time.
   B: Yes, **if there's any justice in the world**.

3. **A:** I'm going to take the dog for a walk.
   B: Fine.
   A: **Unless I wait until later**? Then you can come too.
   B: Sure. I'll only be twenty minutes.

▶ Practice: Exercises 3 and 4 page 79.

> " People often 'add' clauses in detective programmes on TV:
> **A:** The body must have been thrown out of the car around four in the morning.
> **B:** Which is why there weren't any witnesses.
> Listen out for it next time you watch!

Answers

1. 1 awful   2 gorgeous   3 stunning
2. **Possible answers:** She's working really hard, isn't she?, She never stops.
3. 1 Which is rude, isn't it?   2 'Cos I'm going to try that Thai recipe from the internet.   3 Because you've been sitting in front of that computer all day.

18 FOLLOW YOUR PARTNER

Practice

1a Match the sentences 1–8 with the responses a–h.

1 It's so hot outside.
2 The metro carriage was really full.
3 The traffic is awful today.
4 She looked so tired this evening.
5 The drinks are so expensive in that bar.
6 That was absolutely gorgeous food.
7 Her husband is really handsome.
8 Her children are so sweet.

a Cute aren't they!
b Exhausted!
c Boiling!
d Delicious!
e Packed!
f Exorbitant, aren't they!
g Terrible!
h Gorgeous!

b Listen to check your answers. Notice the 'up-down' (↗↘) intonation in the short responses. Listen again and repeat.

2 Complete the dialogues 1–6 with a phrase from the box.

> A *weepy* is a film/book, etc., that makes you cry (weep).

they're so talented • so simple • He was very weird • really life-changing • it's very cosmopolitan • a real weepy

1 **A:** I think Gary's behaving very strangely at the moment.
   B: You're right, I hope he's okay. _____ tonight.

2 **A:** How was the trip?
   B: Fantastic! New York's so interesting, really multicultural.
   A: I know, _____ isn't it?

3 **A:** Did you enjoy the concert?
   B: I thought it was absolutely amazing. Such accomplished musicians.
   A: Oh I know, _____ aren't they?

4 **A:** I found that book so inspiring.
   B: Yeah, I know what you mean, it's _____ isn't it?

5 **A:** That film is so sad.
   B: Yeah, _____, isn't it?

6 **A:** Wow, did you make this delicious cake?
   B: Yeah, it's a Jamie Oliver one, it's really easy.
   A: Jamie Oliver? Oh I love his recipes, they're _____ to make.

PRACTICE

3 Put the dialogues 1–6 in the correct order.

1 a It's a long story. Can you put the kettle on? I really need a cup of tea! _____
   b I've had an awful day. __1__
   c Which explains why you look so terrible! What happened? ___

2 a 'Cos we're off on holiday! The flight's at eight, so I'll go straight from work. _____
   b I'm really excited about tonight! _____
   c I can tell. _____

3 a I'm really confused about this guy I've met. _____
   b I know, I'll tell you one day, but it's all very complicated. _____
   c Whose name we can't mention … _____

4 a Which explains why you're an hour late! _____
   b I'm really sorry, but it wasn't my fault. I tried to ring you! Wait till you hear what happened … _____
   c I've had the most insane morning. _____

5 a I know, but honestly – nobody can survive doing fifteen-hour days for weeks on end.
   b Because you've been working too hard! _____
   c I've had to this week. We had to close a big deal. _____
   d I think I'm coming down with something. I've got a thumping headache and I'm really tired. _____

6 a Well, I also thought I might try the London marathon this year. _____
   b 'Cos I'm going for a run before work. I'm trying to get fit. _____
   c Wow, you're up bright and early. _____
   d What for? _____

> We often use the words *insane* or *mad* to describe how busy or confusing something is.

4 Underline the correct word to complete the dialogues 1–6.

1 **A:** It should be great party tonight.
   B: *If/Unless* your ex turns up and causes trouble again.

2 **A:** I'm just popping to the supermarket for a few things.
   B: Okay, see you soon.
   A: *Unless/If* you want to go instead?

3 **A:** Look at the time! I'll never get to my class on time.
   B: *If/Unless* I give you a lift?

4 **A:** He's a very clever boy, he'll easily pass the entrance exam.
   B: I think he will, *unless/if* he puts his mind to it.

5 **A:** Okay, so let's meet at the pub at eight.
   B: Fine, see you there.
   A: *Unless/If* we get something to eat first?
   B: Actually, that'd be nice, *if/unless* you fancy it

6 **A:** I've had enough of her! She's always so rude to people.
   B: *If/Unless* she wants something!
   A: That's true, she's very nice then. Well, I'm not going to speak to her again.
   B: Good for you! *If/Unless* you can manage it!

> *Ex* is the term used to refer to ex-boyfriend or ex-husband.

Extension

Choose two of the following situations and write a short dialogue, using the repetition techniques from this unit.

1 Describe your journey to work/college today.
2 Discuss an expensive/cheap restaurant that you both know.
3 Chat about a book you've both read or a film you've both seen.
4 Talk about a city you both know.
5 Describe getting a fine or punishment for something.

79

19 PUT IMPORTANT THINGS AT THE FRONT

About the language

> The broken cups, did you throw them away?

In conversation, we can sometimes change the regular order of words to put emphasis on particular parts of the sentence. We focus on this aspect of spoken English in the last two units of this book. First, we look at 'heads': things we take from their normal place and put at the front of sentences.

1 Recognising 'heads'

We often use heads in questions. Here is a question using normal word order:

> Did you wear your new pink dress to Jo's party?

And here is the same question, with *your new pink dress* at the front as a head:

> **Your new pink dress**, did you wear it to Jo's party?

Find three questions with heads in the dialogue below, and <u>underline</u> the heads. Rewrite them in the normal word order. Check your answers on page 81.

Amy:	Thank goodness they've finally gone! It's two in the morning.
Tom:	What a mess! That red bag in the corner, is it yours?
Amy:	Oh no! Someone's left it. The girl with the tall boyfriend, do you know her name? I think it's her bag. They left at midnight.
Tom:	She'll ring us, won't she? Anyway, we'd better start clearing up. Those bottles on the table, are they all empty?
Amy:	Yes. They can be recycled.

🔊(47) Listen to the dialogue and notice the intonation speakers use for the head, and the pause after it.

▶ Practice: Exercises 1, 4 and 5 pages 82–83.

2 The purpose of heads

Try using a head to ask the question below. Check your answer on page 81.

> Is that table by the window free?

Taking something from its normal place and putting it at the front is a way of saying 'This is what I'm talking about':

> A: **My new trainers**, I can't find them anywhere.
> B: Have you looked under the sofa?

In a shop, it's a bit like pointing your finger:

> A: **This DVD player**, is it the cheapest one you've got?
> B: No, madam. But it's one of the most popular.

ABOUT THE LANGUAGE

It is also a useful way of breaking a long or more complex sentence into two parts:

> Are the people you work with nice? → **The people you work with**, are they nice?

And when we're talking about friends of friends, or the family of people we know, it can be easier to understand what we're saying if we use heads:

1 Sal's new teacher's husband is a footballer. → **Sal's new teacher**, her husband is a footballer.
2 My friend Jack's parents are both doctors. → **My friend Jack**, his parents are both doctors.

▶ Practice: Exercises 2, 4 and 5 pages 82–83.

3 'Repeating' the head

Apart from the change in word order, there is another grammatical difference between a regular sentence and a sentence with a head.

Look at the two examples below. What is the other grammatical difference? (If you're not sure, count the words in both questions.) Check your answer below.

> 1 Are those mountains in the distance the Alps?
> 2 Those mountains in the distance, are they the Alps?

After putting a head at the front, we must 'repeat' it later on with a pronoun:

1 **A:** That new French restaurant on Park Street, does **it** look any good?
   B: The menu's interesting, but it's very pricey.
2 **A:** The CDs you bought this morning, can I have a look at **them**?
   B: Of course. I put them on the kitchen table.
3 **A:** The house opposite the cinema, is **that** where you live?
   B: That's right. I see all the latest films.
4 **A:** My mum, **she's** always shouting at me!
   B: I'm not surprised. You never do anything to help around the house.

▶ Practice: Exercises 3 and 4 pages 82–83.

4 The variety of types of head

The examples below show how you can use subjects, objects and clauses as heads:

1 **Denise** is the person you need to speak to. → **Denise** (subject), she's the person you need to speak to.
2 Tom's sold those two old computers, you know. → **Those two old computers** (object), Tom's sold them, you know.
3 I've lost the phone number of **the man who repaired our fridge**! → **The man who repaired our fridge** (clause), I've lost his phone number!
4 Did **the woman in the corner** tell you her name? → **The woman in the corner** (clause), did she tell you her name?

Answers

1 That red bag in the corner, is it yours? (Is that red bag in the corner yours?); The girl with the tall boyfriend, do you know her name? (Do you know the name of the girl with the tall boyfriend?); Those bottles on the table, are they all empty? (Are those bottles on the table all empty?)
2 That table by the window, is it free?
3 When we use a head, we need to use a pronoun in the second part of a sentence to refer back to it.

19 PUT IMPORTANT THINGS AT THE FRONT

Practice

1a Match 1–6 with a–f to make sentences.

1	Your new shoes,	a	it really hurts!
2	That woman by the window,	b	have you met them yet?
3	My foot,	c	where did you get them?
4	The new neighbours,	d	have you still got the recipe?
5	That delicious chocolate cake,	e	what was the score?
6	The match last night,	f	is she a relative of yours?

(48) Listen and check your answers. Then listen again and mark the stressed words and pauses.

2 Complete the dialogues 1–6 with the questions/statements a–f.

1 **A:** _This spaghetti, it's cold!_
   B: I'm very sorry. We'll change it right away

2 **A:** _____
   B: It does. Would you prefer it without?

3 **A:** _____
   B: Oh, it's on special offer, £599.

4 **A:** _____
   B: Sure, anything else?

5 **A:** _____
   B: Oh dear, I'll go and change them for you.

6 **A:** _____
   B: No, sorry, that's the last one I'm afraid.

a The French cheese, I'll have 300g please.
b These apples, they're bruised!
c That red coat, have you got it in a size 10?
d The computer in the window, how much is it?
e The salad, does it come with a dressing?
f ~~This spaghetti, it's cold!~~

3 Choose the correct pronoun (*it*, *him*, etc.) to complete the questions.

1 These papers on the table, are _____ yours?
2 Your new black boots, can I borrow _____ tonight?
3 The new Turkish restaurant, have you been to _____ yet?
4 The actress in that film, I can't stand _____!
5 The woman over there in the fur coat, what's _____ name?
6 The tickets you bought, are _____ really the best you could get?
7 That blue bike over there, is _____ his?
8 The bus stop at the end of the road, is _____ where we have to go?

PRACTICE

4 Rewrite the sentences in two parts using the underlined heads and pronouns in brackets.

1. Could you pass me the jug of water please? (it)
   That jug of water, could you pass me it please?
2. Is the book you're reading at the moment any good? (it)
   _____
3. Are the swimming baths far from the school? (they)
   _____
4. Did you see those amazing documentaries on Africa? (them)
   _____
5. Do you remember the name of the Russian girl in your evening class? (her)
   _____
6. I can't find my memory stick anywhere. (it)
   _____

5a Complete the dialogues with the phrases in the box.

My bike • That man • Michelle Thomas • ~~My mum's birthday~~ • The phone bill • His e-mail

1. **A:** *My mum's birthday*, it's today! I forgot to send her a card.
   B: Why don't you ring her, then?
2. **A:** _____, I forgot to pay it!
   B: But it was due weeks ago. We'll get cut off!
3. **A:** _____, he's so rude!
   B: Why? What did he do?
   A: He never looks at you when he's serving you, never says hello and just throws your change at you.
4. **A:** Can I speak to somebody about my account please?
   B: _____, she's the person you need to speak to. She's at the desk over there.
5. **A:** _____, that guy's just stolen it!
   B: Don't worry, I'll go after him.
6. **A:** _____, it wasn't very clear.
   B: I know what you mean, it didn't answer any of our questions did it?

b Add lines a–f to the dialogues 1–6 above.

a. Thanks, I'll go and speak to her now.
b. I will! As soon as I get a spare minute.
c. No; he's really not a very good communicator.
d. Don't worry; I'll ring them straight away.
e. Be careful! He might get nasty.
f. He obviously needs to go on a training course!

Extension

1 Imagine you're staying in a foreign country. Write a dialogue using headers to ask about the local area. Look out of the window to get ideas (e.g. *That white building, is it a sports stadium?*)

2 Record the dialogue. Remember to stress the correct words and pause, as in Exercise 1.

83

20 PUT IMPORTANT THINGS AT THE END

About the language

> It's too far to go for a week, Japan.
>
> In Unit 19, we explored 'heads'. In this unit, we look at 'tails': things we take from their normal place and put at the end of sentences.

1 Recognising 'tails'

The normal rule in English sentences is to use a noun first, and then to refer to it later with a pronoun:

> **Karen's** got a new job. **She's** going to be working in Leeds.

But people sometimes do it the other way round:

> **She's** got a new job, **Karen**. **She's** going to be working in Leeds.

In the example above, we can call the word *Karen* a 'tail'.

<u>Underline</u> seven 'tails' in the dialogue below. The first one has been done for you. Check your answers on page 85.

Jess: They're rather good, <u>these sardines</u>. How's your curry?
Tim: Actually, I'm not very hungry. I'm feeling a bit tense.
Jess: Well, this is your chance to relax, this meal with me. I know you're worrying about your sister again. But try to be positive. She'll be okay, Sophie will.
Tim: But it was so short, that last phone call she made. And it can be a dangerous city, LA.
Jess: I know, but you're too responsible. I don't have one, a younger sister or brother. But once they're adults, they lead their own lives. You can't wrap them in cotton wool.
Tim: You're probably right. And it tastes lovely by the way, the curry does.

🔊(49) Listen to the dialogue. Notice the intonation used for the tail, and the pause before it.

2 The purpose of tails

Try rewriting this comment about a novel, using a tail. Check your answers on page 85.

> *The Time Traveller's Wife* is a really interesting book.

Tails probably have two purposes. The first is fairly straightforward: we start a sentence with a pronoun (perhaps because it's something we've already been thinking about), and then we want to make sure that the listener understands what it refers to, so we add a tail:

1 It was rather odd, **John's idea.**
2 Have you got one, **a black pen**?

ABOUT THE LANGUAGE

The second purpose is to do with 'managing information'. We can use a tail to hold back a piece of information deliberately, perhaps in order to get someone's attention, before explaining it:

> I'm not sure if he knows what **he** really wants to do, **your friend Steve**.

▶ Practice: Exercises 1 and 2 page 86.

3 The grammar of tails

A tail works by 'expanding' the pronoun (*they, this, she, it, one*) in the main sentence into a full noun or noun phrase in the tail:

1 They're really comfortable, **these jeans**.
2 It was far too long, **that documentary on global warming**

For extra emphasis, a tail can bring a verb form with it, repeating a form of *be*, *have* or a modal verb, or using a form of *do*:

1 She's forgotten her ID card again, Millie (**has**).
2 He would invite the whole world to his party, Peter (**would**).
3 They always give the same answers, politicians (**do**).

But note that we can't do this if the pronoun is the object rather than the subject of the main sentence:

> I don't really enjoy them, **war films**.

Note also that we occasionally use tails and question tags together:

> But it gets really hot in August, doesn't it, Greece?

▶ Practice: Exercises 1–5 pages 86–87.

4 A second type of tail

How is the sentence below different from the examples we've seen so far? What is the purpose of a tail like this? Check your answers below.

> He drives fast, **he does**.

A second type of tail is where the pronoun in the main sentence is simply repeated with a verb form as above or on its own:

> He's a hard worker, **him**.

Note that when subject pronouns are repeated on their own, they become object pronouns:

> We're winners, **we are**. ➜ We're winners, **us**. ~~we~~!

It and *they* are repeated on their own as *this/that/these/those*:

1 It's a lovely drink, **this** ~~it~~.
2 They're gorgeous curtains, **those**.

Full nouns with *be* can also be repeated as full nouns or as pronouns with their verb form, but not normally on their own:

1 Chris is fantastic, Chris is. ~~Chris is fantastic, Chris.~~
2 Chris is fantastic, he is. ~~Chris is fantastic, him.~~

▶ Practice: Exercises 3, 4 and 5 pages 86–87.

Answers

1 They're rather good, <u>these sardines</u>. Well, this is your chance to relax, <u>this meal with me</u>. She'll be okay, <u>Sophie will</u>. But it was so short, <u>that last phone call she made</u>. And it can be a dangerous city, <u>LA</u>. I don't have one, <u>a younger sister or brother</u>. And it tastes lovely by the way, <u>the curry does</u>.
2 It's a really interesting book, *The Time Traveller's Wife* (is).
4 The pronoun is used twice. The purpose is simply emphasis.

20 PUT IMPORTANT THINGS AT THE END

Practice

1 Complete the sentences below using these phrases in the box.

your brother will • husband and me • that sales assistant is • this meeting • this book I've bought • these trousers my mum got me • Budapest • that film

1 That was terrible, _____. You can choose what we go to see next time.
2 I don't think they look very good, _____. I'll give them to a charity shop.
3 It's going to be a great read, _____. Kafka's my favourite writer.
4 We don't like the English winters, my _____. That's why we go away every year.
5 This is our only chance to talk face to face, _____. Otherwise we'll have to e-mail.
6 He's really rude, _____. I think I'll report him to the management.
7 It's a beautiful city, _____. Spring is the best time to visit.
8 Unless he stops smoking immediately, he'll make himself really ill, _____.

2a Underline the correct alternatives to complete the sentences.

1 He was awful, *that man*/*that woman*. He tricked my aunt and stole all her money.
2 It's really delicious, *this ice cream*/*this meal*. How long did it take you to cook it?
3 It really upset me, *Trevor's comment*/*your e-mail*. I wish he'd think before he speaks.
4 I hate them, *spiders*/*bad jokes* – especially if they're big and hairy.
5 It can be a dangerous place, *the park*/*poorly-lit streets*. You don't know who you might come across.
6 She's so good, *my French teacher*/*my piano teacher*. I was speaking like a true Parisian after four weeks!
7 It looks fantastic, *your dress does*/*your kitchen does*. It was worth spending all that money on the pine cupboards.
8 I lost them all, *my wallet*/*my Christmas presents* – when my flat was burgled.

b Match the sentences above with the responses a–h.

a I agree. You really need a bodyguard!
b Thanks very much – it's made a real difference. I actually enjoy cooking now!
c I know! I'm afraid of them, too!
d You poor thing. Let me help you buy some more.
e Wow! I wish I could speak another language fluently.
f All day, actually. But I enjoyed myself.
g He is rather tactless, isn't he? I can't relax when he's around.
h He didn't, did he? How much did she lose?

3 Match 1–6 with a–f to make sentences.

1 I failed my driving test ten times! I'm an idiot,
2 They keep whispering in corners,
3 It's a delicious pudding,
4 Brian is a genius,
5 They're such sweet puppies,
6 You stayed up all night? Well, you've obviously got more stamina than me,

a you have!
b this. You must give me the recipe.
c me.
d those. Can I take them home with me?
e Brian is. He's got an IQ of 250!
f those two. I wonder what they're saying?

PRACTICE

4 Put the words in the correct order to make sentences. Add punctuation where necessary.

1 her / hard / she / works
   She works hard, her.

2 humour / sense / he's / a / of / him / got / great
   _____

3 beautiful / it's / outdoors / this / a / night / be / to
   _____

4 John / John's / a / is / man / lovely
   _____

5 you / than / cleverer / you're / me / are
   _____

6 sleeping / been / I / I've / have / day / all
   _____

5a Put the dialogues in the correct order.

1 a Oh my goodness, that's terribly expensive! Can you do it cheaper? _____
  b It's in a terrible state, your kitchen. It'll cost at least £10,000 to put things right. _____
  c I'm a professional, I am – so I can't do it on the cheap! I can't charge much less; but if you pay cash I'll knock it down to £9,000. _____

2 a You're such an adventurer, you are. Okay, I'll go online and book the tickets. _____
  b I know, but it'll be really worth it, the trip. We can do a bit of touring, too. _____
  c It's such a long way to fly for a wedding, Las Vegas. _____

3 a Oh dear! Let's look for them. I'll go this way if you go that. _____
  b Where's Toby? He's gone and disappeared again, he has! _____
  c I saw him with the neighbour's kids a few minutes ago. You know, Michael and Ben. They're naughty monkeys, those two! They could be anywhere by now! _____

4 a Why's that? Is it getting you down, the weather?
  b I'm really fed up, me.
  c Yeah. It's so cold, and you can't go anywhere in the snow, can you?

50)) Listen and check your answers. Then listen again and repeat, paying particular attention to the use of pause and intonation.

> We often use *on the cheap* as a slightly negative informal way of saying 'inexpensively', and *knock it/the price down* as an informal way of saying 'reduce the price'.

Extension

Using the dialogues in the exercises above as a model, create short conversations with both types of tails. These dialogues might include

describing food
a problem to solve
describing a situation or
forming a picture of someone you know.

87

KEY

Unit 1

1a+b

2 Any <u>messages</u>?   3 More <u>orange</u> juice?
4 Any <u>news</u>?   5 Any <u>phone</u> calls?   6 More <u>sugar</u>?

2

Sue:	That was so delicious! Thanks Phil.
Phil:	No problem. ~~Would you like some more spaghetti?~~ **More spaghetti?**
Sue:	I don't think I can, I'm completely full.
Phil:	Have you had enough to eat Jan? **What about you, Jan?**
Jan:	I'll have a bit more please, if nobody else wants it.
Phil:	Of course, here, help yourself. I'm going to make some coffee. ~~Would you like some coffee too?~~ **What about you?**
Sue:	Yeah, that'd be good, thanks.
Jan:	~~Is there any chance I could have a cold drink please?~~ **Any chance I could have a cold drink please?**
Phil:	Sure. Would you like some coke or juice? **Coke or juice?**
Jan:	Coke please.
Phil:	~~Would you like something cold too, Sue?~~ *What about you, Sue?*
Sue:	No, just coffee's fine, thanks.

3

2 And you?   3 What/How about   4 What/How about you?   5 What/How about   6 how/what about

4

1 e   2 c   3 d   4 b   5 a

5a

1 What's on?   2 Who's it by?   3 What's it about?
4 Who's in it?   5 What time's it on?

b

Isla:	So, what do you fancy <u>doing</u> tonight?
Josh:	I'm not <u>sure</u>. How about a <u>film</u> or something?
Isla:	That could be <u>good</u>. What's <u>on</u>?
Josh:	Actually, there's a new <u>thriller</u> out this week.
Isla:	Oh, okay, <u>Who's</u> it <u>by</u>?
Josh:	<u>Martin Scorsese</u>. Do you <u>like</u> his stuff?
Isla:	I <u>don't</u> really <u>know</u> his <u>films</u>. <u>What's</u> it <u>about</u>?
Josh:	A <u>murder</u> – it's supposed to be <u>really gripping</u>.
Isla:	Well, <u>maybe</u>. Who's <u>in</u> it?
Josh:	Nobody <u>famous</u>. They're all <u>unknown</u> actors.
Isla:	Okay, let's <u>give</u> it a <u>go</u>. What <u>time's</u> it <u>on</u>?
Josh:	<u>Eight-thirty</u> at the <u>Odeon</u>. Perhaps we could <u>get</u> something to <u>eat first</u>?
Isla:	<u>Great</u>. Let's <u>go</u>!

6

2 What's up   3 Any luck   4 What about you   5 How about   6 What's on

Unit 2

1a

2 I don't know where   3 I don't know how.   4 I don't know which   5 I don't know why   6 I don't know when   7 I don't know what   8 I don't know where

b

The two sentences which don't need any information after the gap are 3, 8.

2

2 d   3 c   4 h   5 f   6 a   7 e   8 b

3

1 I think it was   2 I think you should
3 I don't know whether   4 I think it's
5 I think I might   6 I was thinking of
7 I think it was   8 I don't know why

4a

2 A: <u>Oh</u>! What are <u>you</u> doing here? I <u>thought</u> you were going to <u>Trish's party</u>.
   B: <u>No</u>, I didn't <u>feel</u> like it.
3 I <u>thought</u> the <u>audience</u> looked <u>really bored</u> during <u>Roger's speech</u>.
4 <u>Mexico</u>! I <u>thought</u> they were <u>emigrating</u> to the <u>United States</u>!
5 I <u>thought</u> I would <u>look</u> for a <u>new dress</u> in the <u>sales</u>.
6 <u>Jane</u>! I <u>thought</u> you <u>said</u> you <u>weren't coming</u>!

c

1 5   2 2, 4, 6   3 1, 3

5

Becky:	Well, Nuala, this is a very good essay, so ~~I'm not thinking~~ **don't think** you should worry about getting a bad grade. Actually, I ~~am~~ think you will probably get a 2:1 or even a First.
Nuala:	Oh wow, I'm so pleased. I really love Dublin architecture, but I wasn't sure if I could actually say anything worthwhile about it. Becky, while I'm here, can I ask you about my next assignment?
Becky:	Sure, go ahead.
Nuala:	Well, I ~~not~~ **don't** know if you'll agree with this, but I ~~did thought~~ **was thinking** of taking a look at some modern Irish sculpture next – Barry Flanagan's rabbits. I ~~have~~ thought I would try to compare his work with other twentieth-century animal sculptors.

88

KEY

Becky: That's really very interesting, but I thought you ~~say~~ **said** you wanted to specialise in Dublin architecture. That's what you wrote in your proposal.

Nuala: I know, but I think I ~~will~~ **would** like to change that, if it's not too late.

Becky: Well, I ~~didn't~~ **don't** know what the exam board will say about this, but we can ask for their advice.

Nuala: Thanks ever so much.

Unit 3

1

1 F (rising intonation)
2 F (rising intonation)
3 F (rising intonation)
4 U (falling intonation)
5 U (falling intonation)
6 U (falling intonation)

2

2 The ~~really~~ weather in Belgium is really hot at the moment.
3 **A:** Waiter! My food's too spicy!
   B: Sshh! ~~Really~~ do you really want to send it back to the kitchen?
4 **A:** Would you like a piece of cake?
   B: Not really; it will spoil ~~really~~ my diet.
5 **A:** I shouldn't pay this much for a dress.
   B: Well, it's not that ~~really~~ expensive, really.
6 **A:** I don't like dogs.
   B: Really? Where you ~~really~~ bitten by one or something?
7 **A:** Sorry, I must have upset you.
   B: ~~Really~~ no, you didn't really.
8 **A:** I can't stand her!
   B: Oh, come on, do ~~really~~ you really mean that?

3

1 actually   2 actually   3 Of course.   4 Oh, really?
5 of course   6 actually

4

1 really   2 actually   3 Actually   4 of course
5 Actually   6 Really   7 Of course   8 really

5

1 anyway   2 then   3 though   4 though   5 then
6 Anyway   7 though   8 Anyway

6

2 Can you **just** listen for a second while I explain why I didn't call you?
3 I know you think the music's awful, but I **really** like it.
4 **A:** Sorry I took your last bit of money.
   B: I've already told you not to worry. It's okay, **really**.
5 I know you're busy, but couldn't you come **just** for the beginning of the party?
6 **A:** How's Sue getting on with the job-hunting?
   B: **Actually** she's got an interview this afternoon.
7 **A:** Is she your girlfriend?
   B: No, we're **just** flatmates.
8 **A:** Shall we watch the documentary, or do you want to see that new quiz show?
   B: I **really** don't mind what we watch./I don't mind what we watch, **actually**.

Unit 4

1

1 a   2 b   3 a   4 b   5 b   6 a   7 b   8 a

2a

2 full-full   3 full   4 full   5 weak-full-weak
6 full-weak   7 full   8 full-full-weak   9 full-weak

b

1 Ms   2 Doctor (but if the person is also a Professor, use 'Professor')   3 Officer   4 Sir   5 Miss

3

2 dear   3 kids   4 guys   5 Ladies and gentlemen
6 everyone

4a

1 Mrs, Miss   2 madam   3 sir, officer   4 doctor
5 mister, mate   6 professor

5

1 c   2 d   3 f   4 e   5 b   6 a

6

1 Hey guys   2 are we having, everyone
3 having starters, folks   4 you idiot
5 Take it easy, man   6 Come on, Em love,
7 Ladies and gentlemen   8 Certainly, sir

89

KEY

Unit 5

1

1 d 2 f 3 e 4 c 5 a 6 h 7 g 8 b

2a

2 B 3 E 4 E 5 U 6 E

b

Intonation tends to go up when the speaker signals understanding and down to signal a beginning/end of something.

3a

2 Well 3 Right 4 well 5 Right 6 Well

4a

1 d 2 c 3 f 4 a 5 g 6 b 7 h 8 e

b

1 4 2 2 3 8 4 1 5 7 6 5 7 6 8 3

5a

1 speaking of 2 I'll tell you what 3 as I was saying
4 Talking about 5 You mean to say

Unit 6

1a

1 E 2 D 3 B 4 F 5 C 6 A

c

1 f 2 a 3 d 4 b 5 c 6 e

2

2 hope 3 said 4 'm afraid 5 think

3

2 suppose not 3 don't think so 4 guess not
5 'm afraid not

4

1 done 2 that 3 can 4 saying 5 does 6 would
7 done 8 that

Unit 7

1a

1 ✔ 2 ✔ 3 ✘ 4 ✔ 5 ✔ 6 ✘

b

1 Could 2 Couldn't 3 Could 4 Could 5 Couldn't
6 Could

c

1 c 2 f 3 e 4 a 5 d 6 b

2

Hi Kes
I was wondering if you and your family fancied coming over on Sunday afternoon. **We were thinking** of having a barbecue. **Do you think** you'll be able to make it?
Rick

Hey Rick
Thanks for your e-mail. We'd love to come over, but there's a slight problem – Jo's mum's staying with us for the weekend, **if you don't mind** her coming, that'd be great. Also, she won't be able to leave her dog at home, so **would you mind** if the dog comes too? **Hope** you don't think I'm being rude – let me know. Kes

3

2 A: Would you mind if I checked my e-mails?
   B: Sure, no problem.
3 A: Would you mind opening a window for me?
   B: No, not at all.
4 A: Would you call a taxi for me?
   B: Yes, I'll do it now.
5 A: If you don't mind, I'd like to leave the conference early.
   B: Yes, that should be alright.
6 A: Do you mind not smoking in here please?
   B: Oh sorry, I'll put it out.

4a

1 were wondering 2 was thinking 3 hope 4 mind
5 think 6 was hoping 7 don't mind 8 would you

b

b 4 c 7 d 2 e 3 f 1 g 5 h 6

5

A: Oh ~~D~~dear, what have I done with my glasses? Where are they?!
B: Excuse **me** are these yours? I found them on the floor near the toilets.
A: Oh, **thank** you!
B: You're ~~W~~welcome.
A: I'm ~~A~~afraid I'm not very awake today. I've just lost my purse. I'm sure it's somewhere here in the library, but I can't find it anywhere.
B: I've got a bit of time to spare, so I could help you look, if you like.
A: That would be so kind of you. **Could** ~~Y~~you possibly look round those bookshelves over there for me while I check here again? **Sorry** ~~T~~to be a nuisance!
B: I know how it feels to have a bad day. I'll meet you back here in a few minutes.
A: That's great. Thanks much.

KEY

Unit 8

1

1 things   2 Things   3 thing   4 thingies   5 thingy
6 things

2

2 things   3 thing   4 things   5 thing   6 thingy

3

2   A: I got this ~~funny machine~~ **thingummy** for Christmas. It wakes you up and makes you a cup of tea!
    B: Amazing! Wish I had one!
3   A: Did you get a / ~~party invitation~~ **thingy** in the post from Jenny?
    B: Yeah, I got one this morning.
4   A: There was a / ~~special event~~ **thing** in the town square today.
    B: Oh! What was that?

4a

1 c   2 e   3 d   4 a   5 b

b

a 5   b 3   c 4   d 1   e 2

5a

2 or something   3 or something   4 and everything
5 or anything   6 and everything

b

The word *everything* is emphatic and stressed, particularly on the first syllable; sentences have a rising intonation. The word *something* isn't stressed; sentences have a falling intonation pattern.

b

1 E   2 B   3 D   4 C   5 F   6 A

Unit 9

1a

1 T   2 V   3 T   4 V   5 T   6 T   7 V   8 T   9 V   10 T

b

(in any order): 3, 5   4, 7   8, 9   10, 2

2

1 d   2 i   3 g   4 j   5 b   6 a   7 e   8 c   9 f   10 h

3

2 loads   3 a couple   4 Loads   5 loads   6 a couple
7 loads   8 a couple

4a

2 bookish   3 nylony   4 nineish   5 shortish   6 sporty
7 Italiany/Italianish   8 youngish   9 minty   10 greyish

5

1 **I've got to do loads of:** shopping./small jobs around the house./paperwork./things at the office./work this weekend.
2 **I'm feeling a bit:** upset./ under the weather./tired.
3 **I've got to do a couple of:** small jobs around the house./things at the office.

Unit 10

1

2   ~~Are there~~ any of those chocolate biscuits left? The ones in the tin.
3   ~~It's~~ freezing today, isn't it?
4   A: What's the matter? You look awful!
    B: ~~I've~~ got a cold, again.
5   A: ~~Are you coming~~/Are you coming to the party tonight?
    B: Yes, I can't wait.
6   A: ~~Have~~ you got/Have you got a light please?
    B: Sorry, no. ~~I~~ don't smoke.
7   A: ~~So I~~ asked her to marry me!
    B: That's great! What did she say?
8   ~~Have~~ you ever/Have you ever been to San Jose?

2a

1 c   2 d   3 e   4 a   5 b

b

1   A: Really great teacher, isn't she?
2   A: Free on Saturday night, aren't we?
3   A: Happy now, are you?
4   A: Awful weather today, isn't it?
5   A: Terrible play yesterday, wasn't it?

3

2 (so) over-priced   3 to Spain   4 come with you
5 buy Jim a birthday present   6 pay for you

4

2   A: How long is your girlfriend away?
    B: ~~For~~ three days. Fancy coming over one evening?
3   A: Let's go out ~~on~~ Saturday night.
    B: Can't, I'm afraid. I'm working.
4   A: Where has she gone on holiday?
    B: ~~To~~ Spain. Not quite sure whereabouts though.
5   A: Where's he staying at the moment?
    B: ~~At~~ our place.
6   A: How long have you known Annabel?
    B: ~~For~~ ages!

91

KEY

5

Dora: So, what do we need then?
Luis: 1 (We need) Everything really. 2 (I) Think we should stock up because we can borrow my mum's car.
Dora: 3 (That's a) Good point. 4 (We need) All the usual things – bread, cheese. 5 (What/How about) Eggs?
Luis: Yeah. 6 (We've) Run out of eggs, so we'll need a dozen.
Dora: Okay. What about coffee?
Luis: Yeah. 7 (We're) Running quite low. 8 (We) Need a couple of packets.
Dora: 9 (What/How about) Milk?
Luis: 10 (We are) Completely out, so put that down – two litres, yeah?
Dora: 11 (That) Sounds good. What about fruit and veg?
Luis: 12 (We) Need lots. 13 (We've) Got your brother coming, haven't we?
Dora: Yeah. What about tins?
Luis:: 14 (We should/need to) Get a few more. Beans, tuna. 15 (They're) always useful.
Dora: 16 (Have we) Got much pasta?
Luis: Let's see. Oh yeah. 17 (We've) Got a bit, only enough for one though, so let's get more.
Dora: Right, let's see what we've got so far: bread, cheese, a dozen eggs…

Unit 11

1a

2 dozens 3 thousands 4 piles 5 tons 6 masses
7 million 8 masses

b

a 2 b 5 c 7 d 3 e 4 f 1 g 8 h 6

2

1 **A:** Can you have a quick word with a customer about a discount? It'll only take two seconds.
   B: Sure. Put her through, will you?
2 **A:** Stop moaning, it'll only take you two minutes to mow the lawn!
   B: But my back's hurting!
3 **A:** It's already 9p.m. and we've got miles to walk before we get to the hotel.
   B: Okay, shall we try and get a cab?
4 **A:** We've been together for ten years now!
   B: I know, but it only feels like weeks, doesn't it?
5 **A:** Didn't you get my birthday card?
   B: No, but the post is really slow here, things take years to arrive.

6 **A:** That lecture was so boring. It seemed to go on for hours!
   B: I know. I fell asleep at one point.
7 **A:** Can I have a quick word?
   B: Just give me five seconds and I'll be with you.
8 Can you hurry up? You've been in that bathroom for weeks now!

3a

1 endless, absolutely 2 absolute 3 everywhere
4 fortune 5 complete 6 agony 7 massive
8 literally

b

1 absolutely /j/ everywhere 2 absolutely /j/ amazing
4 literally /j/ years

4

1 e 2 d 3 b 4 c 5 a 6 f

Unit 12

1

2 Oh, that's 3 Oh, look 4 Oh, do 5 Oh, that's
6 Oh, when

2

1 Oh yeah 2 Oh no 3 Oh my goodness 4 Oh I see
5 Oh

3

1 Oh/Ah 2 Oh/Oh no 3 Oh/Ah 4 Ah/ Aha
5 Oh well

4

1 d 2 b 3 a 4 c 5 f 6 h 7 e 8 g

5

1 Yuk 2 Ouch 3 Oops 4 Ouch 5 Yuk 6 Ouch
7 Oops 8 Oops

6

1 correct 2 ~~Oops~~ Aah/Ooh 3 ~~Yuk~~ Ooh/Oh 4 correct
5 correct 6 correct 7 ~~Ouch~~ Aah 8 ~~Ow~~ Wow

Unit 13

1

1 h 2 e 3 c 4 a 5 f 6 g 7 d 8 b

2

1 S 2 D 3 S 4 D 5 C 6 C

92

KEY

3

1 So you're Ruby's new boyfriend then?
2 So I'll see you at the station?
3 So you don't drive, then?
4 But we'll still meet in Toronto?
5 But I'll see you on New Year's Eve?
6 So you'll remember to post that birthday card?

4

1 d 2 f 3 a 4 e 5 b 6 c

Unit 14

1

1 d 2 a 3 f 4 c 5 b 6 e

2

1 d 2 e 3 b 4 a 5 c

3a

1 Look, will you hurry up?
2 Listen, don't keep shouting, will you?
3 Well, I don't think you can carry more than 20kg.
4 Okay, you can have some more sweets.
5 Hey, what are you doing here?
6 Oh, I don't think you've given me the right change.

b

1 b 2 c 3 e 4 a 5 d 6 f

4

A bank robber goes to prison for stealing, but he **refuses** to tell the police

where he's hidden the money. His wife telephones him in prison

and **says**, 'Darling, I need to plant the potatoes now. I suppose I'll

have to do dig the garden myself this year.' The robber replies,

'**Hey,** don't touch the garden! That's where I buried the money!'

A week later he's having his lunch and he **gets** another phone call

from his wife, saying, '**Listen**, you won't believe this, but yesterday

seven policemen came to the house and dug up the garden!

They didn't seem happy.' The robber **laughs** for a minute or two,

and then says to his wife, '**Okay,** now plant the potatoes!

5

1 having 2 telling 3 You've 4 Look 5 talking
6 saying 7 said

Unit 15

1

1 e 2 d 3 a 4 f 5 c 6 b 7 h 8 g

2

1 b 2 c 3 e 4 a 5 d 6 f

3a

1 We've got to go to a family reunion.
2 I've got to go to the dentist.
3 You've got to see my new car.
4 I've got to lose weight.
5 He's got to stop smoking.
6 You've got to try that new Indian restaurant.

b

1 I've got to go to the dentist
2 You've got to try that new Indian restaurant
3 You've got to see my new car
4 He's got to stop smoking
5 We've got to go to a family reunion
6 I've got to lose weight

4

1 e 2 c 3 d 4 b 5 f 6 a

5

1 'd/had better 2 've/have got to 3 supposed to
4 supposed to 5 've/have got to 6 had better

Unit 16

1

1 Lovely 2 Brilliant 3 Perfect 4 Great 5 Fantastic 6 Wonderful

2

1 Certainly 2 Absolutely Yeah, definitely
4 Absolutely not 5 Definitely not

3

1 Absolutely 2 Certainly 3 Absolutely not.
4 Brilliant, thanks. 5 Certainly, see you then.
6 Great!

93

KEY

4

2 Has it? Yes, and I bought a new battery only a week ago.
3 Oh, are you? I'm afraid so. I shouldn't have eaten that last cream cake.
4 Couldn't you? No. I was sure I was going to fail the course.
5 Has she really? Yes. She just couldn't rely on him.
6 Oh, aren't they? No. My dad's knees are bad, and my mum's got flu.

5a+b

2 You did <u>what</u>? 3 They did <u>what</u>? 4 He did <u>what</u>?
5 She did <u>what</u>? 6 She did <u>what</u>?

Unit 17

1a

1 you put my keys 2 this great band 3 you're sorry
4 somewhere else to stay 5 her computer
6 in the new place 7 at this website 8 turns up

b

1 e 2 f 3 d 4 b 5 h 6 g 7 a 8 c

2

1 /w/ 2 /w/ 3 /j/ 4 /w/ 5 /w/ 6 /j/ 7 /w/ 8 /j/
9 /w/ 10 /j/

3a

1 clear 2 famous 3 friendly 4 handsome 5 early
6 smooth

b

1 tall and handsome 2 soft and smooth
3 loud and clear 4 warm and friendly
5 rich and famous 6 bright and early

4a

1 d 2 f 3 e 4 a 5 c 6 b

5

1 high, low 2 in, out 3 now, then 4 on, off/off, on
5 up, down 6 here, there

6

1 crackly 2 clear 3 join 4 wet 5 lively 6 hot
7 visit 8 down 9 see 10 get

Unit 18

1

1 c 2 e 3 g 4 b 5 f 6 d 7 h 8 a

2

1 He was very weird 2 it's very cosmopolitan
3 they're so talented 4 really life-changing
5 a real weepy 6 so simple

3

1 b, c, a 2 b, c, a 3 a, c, b 4 c, a, b 5 d, b, c, a
6 c, b, d, a

4

1 Unless 2 Unless 3 Unless 4 if 6 Unless, if 6 Unless, If

Unit 19

1a+b

1 Your new <u>shoes</u>, / where did you <u>get</u> them?
2 That <u>woman</u> by the <u>window</u>, / is she a <u>relative</u> of yours?
3 My <u>foot</u>, / it <u>really</u> <u>hurts</u>!
4 The <u>new</u> <u>neighbours</u>, / have you <u>met</u> them yet?
5 That <u>delicious</u> <u>chocolate</u> <u>cake</u>, / have you <u>still</u> got the <u>recipe</u>?
6 The <u>match</u> last night, / <u>what</u> was the <u>score</u>?

2

2 e 3 d 4 a 5 b 6 c

3

1 they 2 them 3 it 4 him 5 her 6 they 7 it
8 that

4

1 The book you're reading at the moment, is it any good?
2 The swimming baths, are they far from the school?
3 Those amazing documentaries on Africa, did you see them?
4 The Russian girl in your evening class, do you remember her name?
5 My memory stick, I can't find it anywhere.

5a

2 The phone bill 3 That man 4 Michelle Thomas
5 My bike 6 His e-mail

b

1 b 2 d 3 f 4 a 5 e 6 c

KEY

Unit 20

1

1 that film
2 these trousers my mum got me
3 this book I've bought
4 husband and me
5 this meeting
6 that sales assistant is
7 Budapest
8 your brother will

2a

2 this meal   3 Trevor's comment   4 spiders
5 parks at night   6 my French teacher
7 your kitchen does   8 my Christmas presents

b

1 h   2 f   3 g   4 c   5 a   6 e   7 b   8 d

3

1 c   2 f   3 b   4 e   5 d   6 a

4

2 He's got a great sense of humour, him.
3 It's a beautiful night to be outdoors, this.
4 John's a lovely man, John is.
5 You're cleverer than me, you are.
6 I've been sleeping all day, I have.

5

1 b, a, c   2 c, b, a   3 b, a, c   4 b, a, c